Love Surpassing Knowledge

More Than Ramps. Understanding
& Implementing Accessibility

NAOMI GRAHAM

RIVER
PUBLISHING

River Publishing & Media Ltd
info@river-publishing.co.uk

ISBN: 978-1-908393-83-8

Published in partnership with New Wine Trust, www.new-wine.org

MIX
Paper from
responsible sources
FSC® C117931

What others are saying...

'This is a book full of wisdom and hope, drawing on years of experience from within New Wine, and written by someone whose heart is full of love for those who are often excluded.'
Paul Harcourt, National Leader, New Wine

'Naomi is a practitioner and a pioneer who is giving a voice to the often voiceless in our society; those with additional needs or mental health issues. Her writing makes the profound and universal message of God's love something that we can offer to another without stigma and prejudice. This book is ultimately about realising a community in which dignity, humanity and our shared identity as children of God are available to all.'
Rev Will Van Der Hart, Pastoral Chaplain, Holy Trinity Brompton

'The work that Naomi is doing through her charity Growing Hope and the ministry Accessible Church that she oversees at New Wine is extraordinary. Her ability to communicate God's love in an accessible way to all people is an inspiration to see. This book is therefore a must read for anyone asking the big questions of how we can open the doors of the church to create a home for everyone and I honestly can't think of a better teacher than Naomi for such a journey.'
Pete Hughes, Leader of KXC, King's Cross, London

Contents

Glossary

Animal walks involve walking like different kinds of animals, for example like a bear (hands and feet on the floor bottom in the air), a crab (hands and feet on the floor, bottom facing the floor and in the air), a snake (commando crawling), a frog (jumping and crouching). These are all movement activities which help regulate our attention.

Auditory information is processed through receptors in our ears and enables us to hear. Changing tempos, pitches and sudden noises are alerting. Steady, rhythmic noise is calming.

Deep pressure touch is calming and helps us to feel regulated. This could be two hands on someone's shoulders pushing firmly, a hand massage, a big hug, or being wrapped tightly in a blanket.

Fidgets can enable us to keep our attention at a 'just right' level when we're asked to focus. 'Tangles' and 'Twist and Lock Blocks' are good fidgets. The rule is 'this is to help you concentrate, if you throw it I will take it away.'

Gustatory information is processed through receptors on your tongue, enabling your sense of taste. We know that spicy, and strong tastes like lemon and coffee can be alerting and that tastes like chocolate and vanilla can be calming.

Hand over hand is a technique often used to support individuals with physical needs to participate. If you put your hand over someone else's hand you can then enable them to do an activity (for example using glue to stick something down).

Interoceptive information is an internal sense which enables us to know whether we feel sick, hungry or need the toilet.It is closely linked to our emotions.

Movement breaks are really important to help us to maintain our attention and concentration. The more movement we do through heavy work activities which put pressure through our joints and give us proprioceptive feedback, the better. Movement breaks could be: getting up and moving around, doing ten star jumps, carrying something heavy from one room to another, animal walks, pushing the wall and posture preparation.

Multisensory means using more than one sense at once. We understand the world through our senses (sight, hearing, taste, smell, touch, movement, body awareness). It is much easier to process something if more than one sense is involved. The more we use all of these senses when we're teaching, worshiping or praying, the more everyone will be able to engage.

Olfactory information is received through receptors in our nose and gives us our sense of smell.Strong pungent smells and smells like lemon and tea tree are alerting, smells like vanilla and lavender are calming.

Prayer buttons (big point audio record buttons) can be used to voice record a prayer which plays when the button is pressed. For example I might sit with a blanket wrapped tight around me and press the prayer button which says 'thank you God that you surround me and are with me always', others would then lay hands on my shoulder and pray that God would speak to me and I would know him with me.

Proprioceptive input is received through receptors in our joints. It provides our sense of body awareness and enables us to know where our body is positioned in space.Proprioceptive input is done through heavy work movement input through our joints (see appendix 3 for lots of ideas).

Tactile input is process through receptors in our skin and gives us our sense of touch. We know that light, tickly touch is alerting and deep pressure touch is calming.

A *total communication approach* is about enabling individuals to have as much opportunity as possible to understand communication. If we use words together with symbols, signs, gestures or objects our communication will be much easier to understand.

Vestibular input is received through receptors in our inner ear. It tells us which way up and which direction we're moving in which gives us our sense of balance. We know that spinning movement is alerting and linear movement is calming.

Visual schedules can be a really helpful tool to enable everyone to know what is happening when. Different companies provide symbol software online. You can use this to make your service sheets, notices and session plans more accessible for everyone. You can laminate these and use velcro to put them on and off a schedule.

Visual information is received and understood through receptors in our eyes. We know that plain geometric backgrounds are calming and busy, multi-coloured and moving images are alerting.

Introduction

'For this reason I bow my knees before the Father, from whom every family in heaven and on earth is named, that according to the riches of his glory he may grant you to be strengthened with power through his Spirit in your inner being, so that Christ may dwell in your hearts through faith-that you, being rooted and grounded in love, may have strength to comprehend with all the saints what is the breadth and length and height and depth, and to know the love of Christ that surpasses knowledge, that you may be filled with all the fullness of God. Now to him who is able to do far more abundantly than all that we ask or think, according to the power at work within us, to him be glory in the church and in Christ Jesus throughout all generations, forever and ever. Amen.'

(Ephesians 3:14-21)

The love of Christ that surpasses knowledge

One thing I love about Jesus is that his love knows no borders. There is no difference, no similarity, no disaster, no success that can stop the reach of his love. This book is called *Love Surpassing Knowledge* because of the passage in Ephesians 3:14-21. Paul prays that the Ephesians would know the love

of Christ which surpasses knowledge. It is both a prayer
and a challenge that I hope this book brings to you and the
individuals that you interact with day to day. A love that
surpasses knowledge is a love in which relationship with Jesus
isn't about what we know, what we can recite or explain, but
about a a connection with God that is deep in the heart of our
being. I've had the privilege of seeing that deep connection and
relationship in children with disabilities who, in the world's
eyes, may not have knowledge, but in God's eyes have an all-
consuming *knowing* of his love and presence.

This book is about encounter with God through Jesus in the
power of the Holy Spirit. It is about God's heart for all people
to be a part of his kingdom. All people – irrespective of their
ability to walk, dance, write or know. It is a reflection of God's
kingdom and his heart for all people – a constant strand in
the biblical narrative. It's also a practical resource for how to
make our churches and communities accessible for those with
additional needs.

There are lots of individuals and churches who are
pioneering accessibility in their communities. This book both
celebrates what these churches are doing and gives further
ideas and strategies that might be helpful as they expand this.
There are also many churches who have not yet grasped what
accessibility could look like. Sadly, I still hear of many stories
where welcome has not been extended to individuals who may
be seen as different, both within their communities and in
church. I heard recently about a boy with Down's Syndrome
who is ignored by volunteers in the children's ministry because
they don't know how to support him. I have supported a family
who was told they had to leave their rented accommodation

because of their son's additional needs. I have seen communities of adults struggle to welcome and connect with adults with learning disabilities who, when someone takes the time to realise, have so much to offer. I have seen adults afraid of how to respond and welcome individuals with mental health needs into their churches. As God's people, I would love it if this book enables us to expand our welcome in a way which reflects his kingdom.

This book is for everyone. You don't need to have a certain passion for ministry with individuals with additional needs – but it's great if you do! If every church leader, volunteer or individual who is part of a church community could further grasp God's love that surpasses knowledge, and the practical steps we can take to recognise every individual's preferences and needs, we would see a church which more readily reflects God's kingdom.

The first two chapters of this book talk about the things that God puts in us that lead to action and enable us to change the way we do things. Chapters 3–10 explore our sensory processing. We all understand the world through our senses (sight, hearing, smell, taste, touch, balance, movement and *interoception* – an internal sense of feeling sick, hungry etc). Each of us, whether we have additional needs or not, have different preferences in the way we learn and respond to the world around us because of these senses. Chapters 3–10 discuss how God appears to speak through these senses in the Bible and how we can practically support individuals through each of them.

Chapters 11–15 give a summary of ideas specific to certain age groups and then further practical strategies which can be implemented in your setting. The appendices are full of resources which you are free to use and may give you more ideas about how to apply what this book talks about. The glossary (p7) has a list of terms that may be unfamiliar to you and these are emphasised whenever they appear in the text so that you can look them up if you've forgotten.

I am Head of Accessible Church Ministry for New Wine and it is through the United summer gatherings that I first encountered what it looked like to love, include and celebrate the gifts that God gives each and every individual, irrespective of their additional needs. New Wine has a rich history of supporting individuals with additional needs. So much of the experience I have, the stories I will share, and the vision for inclusion, is down to individuals such as Heather Holgate, Kate Wharton and many others from the Our Place teams who set up and grew additional needs ministry at the summer gatherings. I am ever grateful to those individuals who took the step to pioneer and follow God's heart. I am so excited to have been a part of the Our Place teams and the ministry as a whole as we have expanded to enable children, young people and adults with additional needs and their families to be a valued and essential part of New Wine. Most importantly, it is from so many families across the years that we have learnt and developed a successful ministry. I feel privileged to have met countless incredible individuals who have taught me so much about what it is to be loved by God and to reflect that love to those around me. I have changed the names in any stories in this book in order to protect the identity of each individual.

I recognise that I do not have a disability and therefore I don't know fully what it is like to live with something which impacts my ability to participate in everyday life. I have, however, walked alongside several individuals with a variety of needs throughout my life, both personally and professionally. When I was 16 I became a respite befriender for a little boy with Down's Syndrome. At 18 I became a respite foster carer so that I could look after him and take him out, without his parents needing to be there. Professionally, I'm an occupational therapist and I have set up a charity called *Growing Hope* which provides therapy clinics for children and young people with additional needs through the local church (www.growinghope.org.uk).

As an occupational therapist I look at all the things children do every day, such as washing, dressing, eating, playing and handwriting. I look to see if there's anything they find tricky, why they might find it tricky, and how I can help make it easier. I have had the opportunity to meet some incredible children who have told me about their experiences and I've had the honour of being able to journey with them as they developed their skills. As part of my training I have completed a PhD in the experience of play for children with high levels of physical disability due to Cerebral Palsy (a disability where lack of oxygen to the brain impacts physical and cognitive function to varying degrees). This enabled me to see children's view of play and the freedom they have in this.

I come from the perspective that an additional need is anything which impacts upon someone's ability to participate in an activity. That could be a diagnosed disability – a physical or cognitive need, a mental health need, anxiety, depression, a personality disorder, or another need which makes it difficult to engage in a community setting. (For explanations of some common needs please see Appendix 1). It could also be something less 'official' – a bad day, a season of grief, a feeling of difference to those around you.

As God's people we are all part of his family. We are all *'fearfully and wonderfully made'* (Psalm 139:14). We are all precious to God and can receive his *'steadfast love'* that he pours out on us (Psalm 136:1). As Paul writes in Galatians 3:28, *'there is neither Jew nor Gentile, neither slave nor free, nor is there male and female, for you are all one in Christ Jesus'*.

Difference does not matter. We all have a calling to include everyone, no matter what their differences are.

Chapter 1: Sparks

'In the beginning was the Word, and the Word was with God,
and the Word was God. He was with God in the beginning.
Through him all things were made; without him nothing was
made that has been made. In him was life, and that life was the
light of all mankind. The light shines in the darkness, and the
darkness has not overcome it.'
(John 1:1-5)

God spoke and brought life into being. He created the world we live in. All things that were made came through God. *'The word became flesh and blood and moved into the neighbourhood'* (John 1:14, MSG). Jesus came into the world fully human, as the light of the world to all mankind. God's plan all along has been for all people of the earth to be drawn into relationship with him; to be able to walk and talk intimately with him as Adam and Eve initially did in the garden.

Throughout the Bible, God's heart for all people is continually referred to. I love the way that early on in Genesis God makes a promise to Abraham that, *'all peoples on earth will be blessed through* [him]*'* (Genesis 12:3). This is an incredible promise that reveals God's heart that one day all people will have the opportunity to be a part of his kingdom. Paul talks about this in Galatians 3:7-9 when he refers back to this promise and discusses how all those who have faith, both Jews and Gentiles (anyone who isn't a Jew) are children of Abraham. As we read God's word we constantly gain more and more insight into what God's kingdom looks like. Jesus does not just welcome those who he is expected to welcome. The very nature of God's kingdom is counter cultural. It includes women, tax collectors, beggars, Gentiles – individuals who would all have been perceived as on the edges of society. Jesus sees their whole life and he loves what they bring to his kingdom.

Jesus gives us all the command to '*go and make disciples of **all** nations, baptising them in the name of the Father and of the Son and of the Holy Spirit, teaching them to obey all I have commanded you*' (Matthew 28:19-20). Often, when I think about this command, I'm also reminded of Jesus' instruction to his disciples to let their lights shine so that they would be the '*light of the world*' (Matthew 5:14-16). I'm reminded too that in the beginning Jesus was the light that '*shines in the darkness, and the darkness [did] not overcome it*' (John 1:5). As we follow Jesus' command to make disciples we also are like lights in the darkness. We bring his light to places in which it feels like darkness prevails. This always brings to my mind a picture of individual fires like beacons across a dark country. As the fire spreads and you zoom out, these small fires can light a whole village, a town, even a city. The more we share Jesus and pursue God's kingdom purpose in our lives the more we see the fire spread and the land lit up.

This image of individuals starting fires that are a noticeable expression of God's Kingdom is one I cannot shake. I think the closer we are drawn to Jesus the more we have the potential to set fires and see the light shine brighter and further in the darkness.

I love fires. Whenever there's an opportunity for a fire I will be the one suggesting we start one. One New Year's Eve my family came to stay with me in Northumberland and we welcomed in the new year with a fire on the beach. I have an incredible fold-up, all-in-one fire pit and barbeque which is perfect for beach fires. On the drive there I managed to give wrong directions and we missed the normal road to the beach. After going down a slightly more treacherous, pot-hole filled track we eventually arrived at the beach carpark in the dark of the new year's evening. It was at that moment we realised that we were slightly low on phone battery and torches.

The problem with going to the beach in the evening to start a fire, particularly with limited light, is that it's a bit tricky to see what you're doing. This combined with the general difficulty of lighting a fire with a substantial sea breeze, which almost instantaneously puts out any lit match, means a fire on the beach is a bit of a challenge. But always up for a challenge, and several matches and lots of kindling later, we managed to light our fire. It was a satisfying moment seeing those flames and we then had an incredible time of being warm and cosy, eating chocolate, toasting marshmallows and chatting about the year gone by and the year ahead. Our lack of light and difficulty getting the fire going was a seemingly distant memory.

Once the fire had been going a while my Dad and I went for a walk towards the sea. The tide was a long way out so there was probably half a mile of beach between us and the water. The most poignant moment of that evening for me was on that walk. Turning around and looking back up the beach we could clearly see the fire burning brightly. It was mesmerising. We had walked a long way, yet in the darkness the light of the fire stood out. It's amazing how much you notice a fire or a light when everything else is dark. You can't help looking that way. The more we burn like fires for Jesus the more people start to notice.

Even though I love a fire, I don't always find it easy to get them started. I quite often need a firelighter as well as matches to get a fire going. I admire people who are able to light a fire from just a spark! A spark can be defined as *'a small amount of something, such as an idea, that has the potential to become something greater, just as a spark can start a fire.'*[1] Just as a spark can start a fire, there are sparks of ideas or events that happen in our lives that can lead to a fresh understanding and a greater burning fire in our pursuit of Jesus.

I think that making church more accessible to individuals with additional needs – truly valuing and growing a love that surpasses knowledge – is not just for a select few. I believe it comes from a call to really reflect God's heart for all people, which is seen time and again throughout the Bible. God puts sparks of this in all of our lives so that we can set new fires, or brighter fires, that challenge our view of difference and of who we regard as a valuable part of his kingdom.

Stepping into this can be scary. We can get it wrong. We don't always know how to be a light that shines in the way that Jesus shone in the darkness. We will never be perfect in the way we walk through our lives, but God says to us, *'my grace is sufficient for you, for my power is made perfect in weakness'* (2 Corinthians 12:9).

For me, one of the first sparks in my life towards a fire that burned more brightly with a reflection of God's kingdom was an experience of complete misjudgement – one which made

1. yourdictionary.com

me question my own attitude and perspective on disability. As a young teenager I used to help my mum with the local Beaver Scout group (attended by two of my three younger brothers at the time). On one occasion we were expecting a young boy with a disability to come along. I didn't know anything about his needs, other than he used a wheelchair. As the eldest sibling with three younger brothers I have always naturally wanted to care for others (my brothers might describe this as being bossy!) When I heard that a little boy with a disability was coming, I was excited at having a purpose and an opportunity to be able to support someone to participate. My heart was in the right place – I wanted desperately to enable the boy to join in as much as possible – but, in reality my understanding was very limited.

The night arrived when he came along to beavers. We had all the ramps in place in the school hall we used and I was excited at being able to help him participate. The first half went well. He could do 'hello time' and was able to play the games by moving around in his powered wheelchair. When it came to craft time I thought this was my moment to shine. I could enable him to join in where he might not otherwise be able to. I stood opposite him at the table, took his craft from his place and started to write his name. He stared up at me, looked me straight in the eye and said, 'I can write my own name!'

I was shocked. In that moment I felt a whole range of emotions: embarrassment, shame, sadness that I had got it so wrong. In my naivety I had only seen a physical disability and assumed he probably needed support to write his name. This was most definitely not the case.

This was a significant spark in my life that propelled me into wanting to really see people as God has made them. I have been challenged to try and stop myself making assumptions and quick judgements when I meet someone who is in some way different to me. I try and choose to see value; to talk to everyone and always give them the opportunity to communicate to me what is important to them.

Other sparks occur when there is a natural need. Our Place at the United gatherings of New Wine started as a provision for children with additional needs, because there were children coming along who needed one-on-one support to be able to participate in their groups. Often individuals from churches contact me or become interested in additional needs ministry because a child, young person, or adult with an additional need has started coming along to their church. At the United gatherings we launched our adult provision in 2016. This came out of a tangible need to support adults with additional needs to participate in everything that was happening on site. Access is now a successful ministry enabling adults with additional needs to receive support to access the mainstream venues and teaching, as well as a provision enabling adults to participate in accessible seminars in a smaller space if this is what they need. This is an organic start to an additional needs ministry: we see a need and respond to it.

On the other hand, a spark might just be a thought or a moment which sticks in your mind. A challenge you've heard to create a culture where all individuals, no matter what their needs, are welcome.

There are countless other sparks which have occurred at different times in my life and have led to new fires or understanding. Several moments have become sparks which have challenged my view of relationship with Jesus. This has happened through meeting and seeing incredible children, young people and adults with additional needs live their life in relationship with God. Tom has shown me what it is like to worship Jesus with complete joy, abandon and freedom. Sarah has shown me what it is to carry God's presence in a tangible way. James has revealed the contagious sense of enthusiasm he has about learning from the Bible. Jack brings a true sense of welcome to others which goes beyond a surface level 'hello'.

As you've been reading this chapter perhaps there are thoughts, moments or events that you recognise as sparks in your life. I wonder what made you pick up this book? Perhaps you have a tangible need in your church or community and you need a practical resource to learn how to support people. Perhaps you are trying to create a culture of accessibility in order to respond to the need when it does occur. Perhaps you are a parent of a child with additional needs and you long for your church to be more accessible.

Or perhaps it is something totally different. Stop now, take a breath. Ask God to reveal to you those moments which are like sparks. What has he put in front of you or stuck in your memory that is becoming a spark?

Hold onto this, dwell on it, write it down. Don't stop there, keep talking to Jesus about it. Spend time praying about how you can build fires that use that spark. Take the step to see a new light in the darkness that brings more of God's kingdom vision to light.

Chapter 2: Setting Fires

'Immediately Jesus made the disciples get into the boat and go on ahead of him to the other side, while he dismissed the crowd. After he had dismissed them, he went up on a mountainside by himself to pray. Later that night, he was there alone, and the boat was already a considerable distance from land, buffeted by the waves because the wind was against it. Shortly before dawn Jesus went out to them, walking on the lake. When the disciples saw him walking on the lake, they were terrified. "It's a ghost," they said, and cried out in fear. But Jesus immediately said to them: "Take courage! It is I. Don't be afraid." "Lord, if it's you," Peter replied, "tell me to come to you on the water." "Come," he said. Then Peter got down out of the boat, walked on the water and came towards Jesus. But when he saw the wind, he was afraid and, beginning to sink, cried out, "Lord, save me!" Immediately Jesus reached out his hand and caught him. "You of little faith," he said, "why did you doubt?" And when they climbed into the boat, the wind died down. Then those who were in the boat worshipped him, saying, "Truly you are the Son of God."
(Matthew 14: 22-32)

When we sense a spark, or something that is pushing us closer towards God's kingdom, we need to be ready to set the fire; ready to move from the place of feeling prompted, to acting on that prompting.

In the passage above in Matthew 14 we see Peter take the bold step out of the boat to walk on water. Paul and Becky Harcourt have written an excellent book called *Walking on Water* which is about 'getting out of the boat' in the supernatural and overcoming the obstacles in our heads and hearts that can prevent us from stepping out. They remind us of Jesus' encouragement to Peter to '*come*'. With that single word Jesus invited Peter to step into *more*, into the impossible, into the supernatural.

There are times when stepping into a deeper understanding of God's kingdom for *all* people – those who are similar to us and those who are different – can feel like stepping out of the boat into the unknown. Jesus walked through life fully human, yet able to love and welcome those who were perceived as being on the edges of society. However, this is something we often find hard. We live in a society where there is an ingrained hierarchy – an increasing trend of '*me first*'. Our culture celebrates individualism, which turns life in on itself and prevents people from looking outwards. We need a supernatural shift to enable us to step away from that individualistic perspective and to notice the value that God places on those who are different to us. We have a constant invitation to step into a deeper relationship with God through his son Jesus in the power of the Spirit. It's the Holy Spirit who highlights those sparks, those prompts to set fires which shine in the darkness and become beacons for a culture which openly reflects God's kingdom.

We have an invitation to step out of the boat, to recognise and take the sparks we have noticed, and to grasp the potential for them to become something greater. We can go one step further and set a fire. When Jesus was walking on water, he told the disciples to *'take courage, do not be afraid'*. Peter decided to take a step further than the other disciples and put his trust and faith into action, following Jesus' command to *'come'*. It is not enough to know what God has sparked in us. We need to be prepared to lay the kindling and set fires.

It is a brave thing to choose to step out the boat; to choose to hold onto a prompting and allow it to become something greater. It's brave but essential. Essential if we are to cultivate a way of living which reflects God's kingdom with a heart for all people of all nations and backgrounds to be valued as part of his family.

When you set a fire you not only need a spark, you need kindling and some fuel in order for it to burn. When we step into additional needs ministry we need to have those resources in place that will enable us to set fires which burn brightly and have a big impact. Just as it takes time to chop up a log into pieces small enough to use for a fire, it can take time to prepare and put in place the resources to create a culture in which everyone is welcomed and valued. The rest of this book looks in more detail at different practical resources and strategies that we might use as we start to light those fires.

Stepping into action

A spark is just a spark. If there is nothing for it to set alight it cannot continue to burn. It will not reach the greater potential that it has. It's the same with the spark of ideas that move us towards ministry shaped by God's vision.

We see individuals throughout the Bible step into action through obedience, following the call God has given them. God called Abraham to go from his country to a land that God would show him. He promised him that *all* families of the earth would be blessed by him. Genesis 12:4 reads, '*So Abraham went as the Lord told him*'. Abraham was obedient to the call God placed on him. He caught the spark, the vision, the idea, and stepped out in the direction he felt prompted. I wonder how often we follow God's call on us with immediate obedience? As you go through this book, this is an opportunity to begin to put in place the ideas you've had and the resources that are suggested here, so that you can cultivate a more accessible culture.

Often it is at a conference, such as New Wine's United summer gathering, where you have a spark of an idea. There may be a moment that challenges you or a thought you can't shake. It's not just about recognising these sparks, it's how we set the fires to respond to the challenge God has put in front of us. New Wine is about local churches changing nations. We don't just want individuals to experience excellent additional needs support and provision at our summer festival. We want everyone to be able to experience such support and provision throughout the year. I am so encouraged by the increase that we are seeing in this. So many churches across the nation are now living out and embodying Jesus in the way they welcome, support and value individuals with additional needs in their communities.

I have been to churches where a spark has been created because of a child or young person with additional needs attending their church. This has led to children's and youth pastors training all their team and changing parts of their ministry, so that it becomes accessible to individuals with additional needs. That ministry has then grown and these churches have seen more and more families with additional needs become part of their community. I have also seen individuals who have been a part of the Our Place and Access teams at the United summer gatherings take the spark and set a fire in their churches. Even in places where individuals with additional needs do not yet exist in their communities, churches are shaping and creating a culture in which anyone who comes will be welcome.

In one church the spark originated from a group of parents of children with additional needs, who gathered together for mutual support. This led to the development of a ministry supporting children with additional needs in their church. The first steps to making church more accessible to their children was simply to spend about £40 on sensory objects from IKEA. This formed the basis of a "treasure chest" of rewards and fidgets that enabled everyone to join in. As group leaders found the children to be more engaged, some of them gained a heart for ministry amongst people with additional needs, often preferring to support individuals on a one-to-one basis, rather than with the large group of children. No one felt that they were an expert, but the church quickly realised that parents are often experts in explaining their children's needs and behaviours, and everyone learned and grew together. A few years down the line this has become a thriving ministry for children with additional needs which meets every week, and is a significant aspect of the church's outreach.

There might be times, as well, when a spark leads to a significant action for you and your life. For me there were several sparks in my life which led to my career as an occupational therapist: my experience of Our Place at New Wine; being a respite foster carer for Tom who has Down's Syndrome. I became an occupational therapist because I knew that would equip me to support individuals with additional needs to gain independence and skills in the areas which were important to them.

Perhaps the spark that you have experienced is leading you into this kind of ministry full time? This could be a profession, such as occupational therapy, physiotherapy, speech and language therapy, or counselling. Or it could be a role within your church or community that enables you to create a culture and live this out in a way that burns brightly for God's kingdom.

Whatever the spark is, Jesus calls us to 'come' to take the step, to set the fires that enable the spark to become something greater.

What does it look like to set fires?

We want to be able to set fires that reflect God's heart and kingdom. When we look at the Bible, as we'll see throughout the following chapters, there do not seem to be any occasions where Jesus singles out a person or a group of people to be separate from everyone else. In fact, he does the opposite: Jesus creates a culture where everyone is included. He has dinner with his friends and invites individuals like Zacchaeus, the tax collector. He speaks to people he's not expected to speak to and enables them to be welcomed back into the community.

I was listening to a commentary recently about the Samaritan woman at the well in John 4. Jesus speaks to her of 'living water' and tells her about her history: 'The fact is, you have had five husbands, and the man you now have is not your husband'. The woman then goes back to her community saying, 'Come, see a man who told me everything I've ever done. Could this be the Messiah?' The amazing thing about this sentence is that this woman had a deep experience of Jesus' grace. She would have been shunned by society, someone who existed very much on the edge. Despite this, her encounter with Jesus left her with a deep awareness of the life he brings; of the reality that she was accepted and forgiven; that despite what others thought of her, she could now be a part of the community. She realised that her community didn't need to shun her, because Jesus had welcomed her. She was empowered to communicate with them and be a part of their lives.

I long for a world where there isn't an 'in' crowd and an 'out' crowd; where an additional need doesn't automatically put someone on the edge. This is the kind of world and culture that Jesus models and that we can choose to create as we set fires.

How can we practically respond?

One of the most important things about creating a more accessible church for individuals with additional needs is to ask each individual (or their carer) what would be helpful for them. Appendix 1 has an additional needs form which might help you gather that information.

Throughout this book you'll notice that whenever I refer to someone with additional needs, I do so by first referring to the person, rather than their additional need. Often individuals, and their parents/carers, find it upsetting when they are referred to as 'the disabled man' or 'the Down's boy' etc. God loves and values each of us as we are, therefore we should always refer to the individual first! Thinking about our language is a really simple step which can make a big difference.

Secondly, it is important to develop our awareness of what might be helpful for different individuals. There are several practical, physical things we can put in place to make sure that our churches are accessible. This includes hearing loops for individuals who are deaf; ramps which are no steeper than a 1:12 gradient; accessible toilets (which are kept clear of spare wheelchairs, bins etc., so they are actually accessible). Accessibility is, however, much more than this. There are many more practical considerations that will enable *everyone*, no matter what their needs, to participate in church. That is what the rest of this book is about.

As an occupational therapist I have been able to learn about sensory processing. Sensory processing is a term which refers to the way in which we take in sensory information to our bodies, process it, then apply it to what we are doing. We have five senses which most individuals are aware of – our sense of sight, smell, taste, hearing and touch. We also have three additional senses which are less well known. Our sense of *proprioception* is our sense of body awareness – our subconscious awareness of where our body is positioned in space. Our *vestibular* sense is our sense of balance, which tells us which way up we are and which direction we are moving in, if we are moving. Recent research has also suggested an eighth sense called *interoception*. Interoception enables us to feel and understand messages from inside our body such as hunger, pain, feeling sick and needing the toilet.

Visual (sight)

 Olfactory (smell)

 Gustatory (taste)

 Auditory (hearing)

 Tactile (touch)

 Vestibular (balance)

 Proprioception (body awareness)

 Interoception (internal sensations)

Although on the surface our senses seem very straight forward, they involve a complex network of neurons in our body and they are the foundation of everything we do in our everyday lives. I love that God has created us with incredible brains that enable us to process, understand and respond to the world around us. If we all learn more about these senses and the way that God has created them and speaks through them, both in the Bible and in our own day to day, we are more likely to know how to adapt everything we're doing so that more people are welcome.

Chapters 3-10 will look at how we practically respond to and understand the sensory needs of each individual we come across. We will take in turn each sense mentioned above and look at where God speaks through this sense, or Jesus uses this sense for teaching in the Bible. We'll then look at how we can use and apply that to everyday life. This will help us to deepen our understanding of both our own sensory preferences and the preferences of those around us.

I am praying that this resource enables you to take the steps to create something greater and set fires from the sparks that you have recognised. As we reflected at the beginning of this chapter, a spark is just a spark unless we set a fire and enable it to burn. As we step out of the boat it will not all be plain sailing – we will make mistakes (I'll share some of mine in the coming chapters) – but we will be drawn ever closer to creating a culture which reflects God's kingdom. My hope is that we can capture something more of God's heart and then share that with those around us.

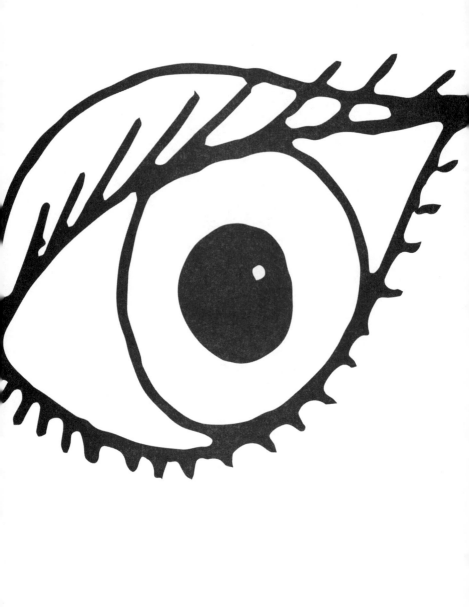

Chapter 3: Seeing Differently
Understanding Our Visual Sense

'Therefore I tell you, do not be anxious about your life, what you will eat or what you will drink, nor about your body, what you will put on. Is not life more than food, and the body more than clothing? Look at the birds of the air: they neither sow nor reap nor gather into barns, and yet your heavenly Father feeds them. Are you not of more value than they? And which of you by being anxious can add a single hour to his span of life? And why are you anxious about clothing? Consider the lilies of the field, how they grow: they neither toil nor spin, yet I tell you, even Solomon in all his glory was not arrayed like one of these. But if God so clothes the grass of the field, which today is alive and tomorrow is thrown into the oven, will he not much more clothe you, O you of little faith? Therefore do not be anxious, saying, "What shall we eat?" or "What shall we drink" or "What shall we wear?" For the Gentiles seek after all these things, and your heavenly Father knows that you need them all. But seek first the kingdom of God and his righteousness, and all these things will be added to you.'
(Matthew 6:25-33)

As we set fires for God's kingdom and start to live our lives reflecting his love for everyone, we start to see things differently. We start to see the way God sees – to look on every individual and recognise the value they have in God's eyes.

Our sense of sight is received through our eyes. We take in *visual* information and process this in our brain. We all have different ways of seeing. Even if we have limited physical vision, we have a way that we perceive and 'see' the world around us. Let's choose to see differently; to look beyond the challenges that additional needs might bring; to love, first and foremost, and value every individual we encounter.

From the moment I tried to write the little boy's name for him at beavers onwards, I had a shift of perspective. I feel like I'm on a constant journey of trying to see things the way God sees them. There is another young boy, Caleb, who I've worked with as an occupational therapist. When I first met him he was unable to make eye contact with anyone. He was unable to respond to his name and found it very difficult to be near other people. Through occupational therapy, speech and language therapy, and an amazing amount of love and dedication from his mum, we saw a significant shift in the way he 'sees'. Caleb is now able to respond to his name, make eye contact and share a smile when he is enjoying something. It has been so precious to see Caleb learn to see the people around him who love him. To not just see with a fleeting glance, but to be able to hold a gaze, to share, smile and laugh with the joy of seeing differently. It is an incredible privilege to have been able to walk with him and his family as we've seen this shift. As I've watched him learn I've seen the creativity, energy and joy that Caleb brings to the world, despite his high level of disability.

One practical way in which we can learn to see differently is to think about how introduce ourselves to the people around us. When we see someone who is different to us, do we choose to look away, to walk away and disengage because we are fearful of what might happen or of what they might say or do? Or do we choose to ask God to enable us to see differently, as he sees, to look beyond what we see in an initial glance? This week you could choose to say hello, to smile, and to ask how someone is doing when you encounter someone you perhaps wouldn't usually talk to. If you chat to someone in your church community you could write down their name and something about them (I often do this in the notes on my phone). Then, next week, you can welcome them and remember their name.

I started making a concerted effort to do this a couple of years ago. I found that as I consistently chose to chat to people I wouldn't normally chat to, to have a conversation that went beyond an initial hello, I started to see differently. I became less afraid of chatting to individuals I didn't know and I also found that more people started to approach me to say 'hi'. Sometimes when we're afraid of the response of others we become so insular that we manage to only make eye contact and engage with the same few people we know. Let's choose to look up, to look out beyond our usual social circles, and to notice those around us.

Another practical way that we can see differently is through the way that we share Jesus with those around us. Whether this is when we communicate our faith on a Sunday, in a small group setting, or through a one-to-one conversation, we can think about how we're enabling others to see the love God has for them. The passage in Matthew 6 from the start of this chapter gives us a practical example. Jesus chooses to use a *visual* illustration to enable people to understand what he means. In Matthew 6:26 Jesus says,

'Look at the birds of the air; they do not sow or reap or store away in barns, and yet your heavenly Father feeds them. Are you not much more valuable than they?'

Let's just dwell on this for a second. We know that Jesus is outside, he has been followed by a crowd and is sitting down on a mountain talking to his disciples. This is towards the end of the sermon on the mount. He commands them to *look at the birds of the air*. This is an instruction to *look* rather than take a fleeting glance. I expect Jesus wasn't hurrying past this instruction – he was taking the time to enable people to see differently, to see more clearly, by using something *visual* to support his words.

I saw some similar *birds of the air* when I was in India. I was up a mountain visiting some families in a slum with children who have disabilities when I saw the breath-taking sight of several eagles soaring around at the top of the valley. Eagles are able to fend for themselves but, like Jesus says, they don't sow, reap or store away. They have to trust that they will get the food they need when they need it. For me, the contrast between the eagles having their needs met and the conditions the families I met in the slum were living with was stark. The families were more valuable to God than the birds, yet they needed to be able to trust Jesus to provide for their everyday needs.

You can probably picture an eagle or bird in your mind. As you do that, reflect on the way God enables these birds to fend for themselves and live. Reflect back on God's promises over you and his unconditional love for you. How does that help you to see and live out your trust in God to meet your needs? Perhaps now, when we see and consider the birds, it will be a reminder to us of the trust we can have in Jesus. This is one way that God can teach us, drawing us deeper into relationship with him.

So how can we use our sense of vision practically within our ministries? Remember that the more clues people receive about the information we're giving them, the easier it is for them to process and learn. When Jesus pointed to the birds and then the lilies, he was giving the disciples something practical. He used something they often saw, on which they could pin the teaching he was giving them. Each time we are teaching or having a conversation about something we'd like to help someone remember, we can think about using their sense of vision. We could describe a *visual* illustration that they can imagine in their mind, or we can provide something visual they can look at. PowerPoint slides and photos are great and a good start in enabling everyone to see what we're saying. However, we can go one step further and bring objects that people can see, touch and feel. We could even go somewhere where people can physically see. If your church has a garden why not go there to think about and learn from Matthew 6:25-33? Going outside to look at the birds and the grass may give an increased realisation of God's provision for us.

Each time you teach, why not spend a few extra minutes thinking about what the teaching could look like. At the very least, use an image and a visual description to enable everyone to picture what you're referring to. Be creative! Think of different ways that individuals may be able to see and experience vision as we think about seeing in the way that God sees.

Research suggests that busy, colourful and patterned visual information can alert and sometimes distract us. Plain, geometric and simple visual information can be easier to process. Think about how individuals may respond to the visual information we present to them. One example of this is that individuals with autism often have incredible visual perception. I saw a documentary a few years ago where the producers filmed some research. It found that adults with autism had significantly better visual perceptual skills and could find a 'Where's Wally' on a large canvas, several metres long, much quicker than adults who didn't have autism.

A visual strength like this can mean that visual information can be distracting. For this reason it can be helpful to arrange the space so that you have limited visual distractions on the wall behind you while you're talking, and to think about what visual cues can support what you're saying. It can be helpful for some individuals to sit nearer the front, where there is less visual distraction between you and them.

As we learn to use practical visual illustration to help everyone see and understand, and as we choose to see everyone with God's eyes, things will start to change in our community. As I grew up I saw this happen in my home church. We had a couple in our church who were foster carers for an individual who used a wheelchair and had a significant physical disability. A few years on, I became a respite foster carer and started to bring Tom to church occasionally. Then, as a church we became more involved with the additional needs provision at our local holiday club. Following that we saw an increase in families who had children and young people with additional needs feel welcome and come and participate in church. What has been interesting is that this has led to a shift in perspective – a way of seeing differently that has permeated the church community. I love the fact that the children who were young at the point when we began welcoming everyone in church, are now teenagers who see differently themselves. They are able to look beyond the differences on the outside and choose to see the way God sees. They welcome individuals who may not naturally 'fit' in their youth group, whether that's because they have an additional need or are from a different school. I have been so encouraged to see the way that many of these teens are so willing and eager to be a part of the Our Place provision for children and young people with additional needs at the New Wine summer gatherings.

Communities can be steadily transformed as individuals choose to see differently. In my church in London, as we have increasingly welcomed individuals with mental health needs, who may not have a permanent address, we have started to see an increasingly diverse community in which it is accepted that everyone is welcome. We still have a long way to go in seeing differently, but the choice of a few to start seeing and valuing individuals who appear to be different starts to shift something.

Seeing differently can often be a big challenge for us. I distinctly remember my first encounter with adults with significant learning disabilities and mental health needs. As part of exploring occupational therapy as a potential career I went for work experience to see what adult occupational therapy was like. In an acute inpatient mental health ward I was initially fearful. I didn't know how to respond, how to see the individuals I encountered. I met an older lady, Vera, with late stage dementia who would take her clothes off, climb on chairs and speak in the language she had spoken as a child (which wasn't English). I didn't know where to start in order to communicate and interact with her, let alone see her in the way that God sees her. I'm sure I was like a rabbit in the headlights. I was a young, inexperienced work experience student who was eager to please and learn, yet absolutely clueless.

Instead of looking at Vera, the individual I was learning how to care for, I spent my first few hours looking at the other individuals in the room – the health care professionals who had experience and knew what they were doing. I found that as I watched the professionals do their jobs, they enabled me to shift my gaze from them to the individuals we were supporting. I learnt to see Vera in a new way. I saw the unrelenting value and care that each professional had for the individuals they were working with. No matter how many pads they had to change, clothes they had to put back on, how much calming language they had to use, they valued the individual.

The majority of my experience is with children and teenagers with additional needs and there are still many times in which I feel afraid or nervous about how I see and interact with adults with significant additional needs. The lesson I learned from meeting Vera was that the best way to learn and gain experience is to put ourselves alongside others who are more experienced in caring for and supporting those with additional needs. This enabled me to start to see the people I came across in a way which wasn't based upon snap judgements, but that chose to look beyond the outward (perhaps hard to understand) additional needs. It taught me to choose to see and value the treasure in every individual, just as Jesus does.

As we ask God to help us to see as he sees, we start to adjust our vision. As we do this we can learn to see the value of individuals and also to be safe in the way that we love others and draw them in. What do I mean by this? When we are working with individuals who are vulnerable, it can be easy to see and love like Jesus, but then slip into an unhealthy feeling of responsibility for another individual's wellbeing. Particularly with adults who have mental health needs or chaotic lifestyles, we need to make sure that we carefully consider their needs and the impact this may have on their interaction. Seeing individuals with the value that God places on them is very different to seeing yourself as responsible for them and for their well-being.

Jesus modelled healthy boundaries and support for the individuals he encountered in the communities he ministered to. For example, when Jesus encountered the woman at the well in John 4, he showed her that he knew her and loved her. This enabled her to know that she was valued and could be a valuable part of her community. Jesus told the parable of the Samaritan man who cared for the wounded individual by handing him over to others who could support him, rather than waiting for him to heal and taking responsibility all on his own. Jesus regularly took time out to retreat with his Father. He was constantly connected to God, but showed us how we can be both in relationship with God and a part of our community.

God continually draws us into community. Throughout the Bible we see the importance of community emphasised again and again. In Corinthians 12:12 Paul talks about the body of Christ saying, *'Just as a body, though one, has many parts, but all its many parts form one body, so it is with Christ'*. We are all parts of one body. We are able to love, value, welcome and see as God sees by working together. It is not about one individual taking responsibility for seeing as God sees, then trying to be entirely responsible for the needs of others. It's about being a part of community.

We can support our volunteers and build community together in a way that enables everyone to stay safe. This can be through simple practical steps, such as only enabling vulnerable adults to have a work contact number for particular individuals. This can help to prevent over-reliance and limit the responsibility a volunteer has for an individual. Steps such as giving a good level of training to volunteers who are coming alongside vulnerable adults can help everyone put healthy boundaries in place. Encouraging the whole community to step up their welcome and, for example, to chat with and welcome individuals they may not previously have spoken to on a Sunday, is a practical outworking of seeing the way God sees.

As church communities step into seeing differently and welcome everyone as Jesus welcomes them, we need to put practical support mechanisms in place. Safeguarding policies and procedures are an absolute necessity for any church and community supporting children, young people and vulnerable adults. Well meaning individuals can easily start to feel responsible for the individuals they encounter, even though their hearts are in the right place. If we have safeguards in place we can enable everyone to learn and grow in seeing the way that God sees, but with healthy boundaries and the support of the whole community.

This can be challenging and is sometimes difficult to manage in terms of pastoral care, but it is possible. In one of my previous churches, Daisy, a lady with significant mental health needs, is supported practically by several individuals from the church community. She only has access to a couple of work numbers and she knows that she can leave a voicemail and someone will get back to her. She needs a lift to church each week and there is a rota of individuals who regularly pick her up and use that time to chat to her and support her. When Daisy is at church, several individuals know her and welcome her in. Daisy is also supported to attend a midweek lunch group which enables her to be part of the church community alongside others. She has needed support to learn practical tasks, such as how to wash and look after herself, but she is a valued, loved part of the church community. Daisy teaches others what it is to see as she sees, and she is very grateful for the support she receives. She often recognises and openly encourages individuals who may not always receive encouragement.

Seeing differently requires us to take time to tune in and ask God to enable us to see things as he sees them. As we do this we can recognise and more readily respond to the needs of the individuals around us. Perhaps this week we can ask God to help us to see differently; to look beyond an individual's additional needs and see as God sees; to value everyone we come across. Then we can practically meet individual's needs in ways that also helps them to learn and see. We can follow Jesus' example of telling the disciples to *look at the birds of the air* and use visual illustrations to enable others to learn more easily.

Chapter 4: Recognising God's Voice
Understanding Our Auditory Sense

'I am the good shepherd; I know my sheep and my sheep know
me – just as the Father knows me and I know the Father – and
I lay down my life for the sheep. I have other sheep that are not
of this sheep pen. I must bring them also. They too will listen
to my voice, and there shall be one flock and one shepherd. The
reason my Father loves me is that I lay down my life – only to
take it up again. No one takes it from me, but I lay it down of
my own accord. I have authority to lay it down and authority
to take it up again. This command I received from my Father.'
–Jesus
(John 10:14-18)

As we desire to see the way that God sees and to share the
love he has which surpasses knowledge, we can increasingly
recognise God's voice. In John 10, where Jesus declares that
he is the good shepherd, he makes it clear that his sheep will
recognise his voice. Earlier in the chapter Jesus says, *'he calls*
his own sheep by name and leads them out. When he has bought
out all his own, he goes on ahead of them, and his sheep follow
him because they know his voice.'

Jesus is using a well-known everyday activity to help his disciples understand the importance of recognising God's voice. In the context of Jesus' middle eastern culture it would have been usual for a flock of sheep to know the particular call of their own shepherd. This meant that if shepherds met on a hillside they could use their unique call to go direct their sheep and lead them forward, enabling them to keep separate from the other shepherd's sheep. Jesus is saying that he has a particular call that he speaks over us that we can get to know and follow. Jesus lays his life down and takes it back up for us, his sheep. He has one flock of individuals, some who are from different sheep pens, but all of whom are welcome as one flock in his kingdom.

As we step further into being a church for everyone, we can take time to listen to and respond to God's voice. Sometimes our response to his voice may not be a cognitive thought-through response. We may perceive God saying something in our mind through a thought, a phrase or a feeling. Whether we can physically hear or not, we are able to 'listen to' and respond to God's voice.

Our sense of hearing, our *auditory* sense, comes through receptors in our ears which enable us to hear and process the sounds around us. We know that fluctuating tone, rhythm and pace can alert our auditory system and that regular paced, calm, rhythmic sounds can be calming. This is why it can be helpful to drop your pitch and volume and use regular language to quieten and 'draw in' a room you're talking to, rather than talking loudly and quickly. The more quietly we talk, the more people lean. This is a great technique to use when story telling! We see this in the way that God speaks to Elijah in a whisper and it might be something you've noticed at church.-If others are talking loudly and you talk quietly, everyone leans in to hear you. Sometimes we need to be tuned into hearing the whispers God speaks. We need to be open to understanding and seeing the different ways in which we can hear his voice.

While we can choose how we respond to the things we hear, for some individuals it's easier than others. In one church there is a family whose teenage daughter, Emily, developed Tourettes and would shout out randomly and sometimes inappropriately in church. Instead of perceiving her shouting and responding as negative, the church family were able to model that it's okay to be different. There was one Sunday when the kids pastor was at the front with the pre-schoolers and Emily shouted out loudly just when it had become really quiet. One of the four year olds leapt up to see who it was who was shouting. He appeared to be about to comment loudly himself, but then realised that no one else in the church had reacted, so he closed his mouth, turned around and got on with what he was doing. We can accept the different ways in which people communicate and process noise as part of being a church family that welcomes everyone.

Jesus regularly taught his disciples by talking to them. They were able to hear what he was saying and they recognised his voice and his teaching. But Jesus didn't just use his voice, he helped them to understand by showing them what he was teaching them about. In the previous chapter we saw that Jesus instructed his disciples to 'look at the birds' when he was encouraging them to trust in his provision. Jesus was using what healthcare professionals term a *multisensory approach* – using more than one sense at once to enable individuals to understand what we are doing. We all process the world through our senses, so the more input we have through these senses about what we are trying to learn, the easier it is for us to do so. If we have difficulty concentrating, or have a learning disability, or can be distracted by hearing voices, we will be more able to listen and understand what is said to us if it's communicated in more than one way.

Speech and language therapists often talk about a *total communication approach*. The idea behind this is similar: if we can communicate what we're saying with both language and something *visual* (such as sign language or a picture) an individual will more easily be able to pick up and understand what we are communicating. We know that a large percentage of the way that we give and receive communication happens through our body language, not just through the way that we talk.

When we do talk, we can think about the language we're using. We are much more able to respond to a request if someone says our name first. If you say, 'Come and sit down over here because it's time to start the story, Naomi', I may only know you are talking to me when you say my name. If you say, 'Naomi, it's time for sitting' and give me a visual cue, such as a hand on my shoulder or a pat on the floor where you'd like me to sit, I'm much more likely to respond. This is particularly the case if I have a learning disability or struggle with attention.

Knowing God and living in relationship with him isn't just about learning in a conventional sense through what we hear. It's a fine art to create opportunities for all individuals, no matter what their cognitive ability, to be able to learn. We can create a balance of teaching with a *multisensory* approach and use complex concepts that stretch and grow those who are more cognitively able. We'll talk about how this can be done corporately with adults in Chapter 13.

So how do we recognise God's voice? I would suggest that because God has created us as individuals who understand and respond to the range of senses around us, we can hear and understand his voice not just through our auditory sense (the sounds we receive through our ears). We can be open to listening to God in different ways and also enable others to hear what he is saying in different ways.

The sheep who learn to respond to and recognise their shepherd's voice in John 10 probably pick up on other sensory clues: how fast the shepherd walks away from them; the way that he touches them; the way that he looks.

We can apply this to the way that we pray and teach others to pray. A multisensory approach means that God can speak deeply to our hearts through any of the senses he's created within our bodies. God can speak to us through what we see, hear, smell, taste, touch, how we move and what we sense within our bodies. This is such good news! I love that God has created us in this way, because it means we don't have to understand cognitively in order to hear and respond to God's voice. We don't have to be able to learn what he is saying to us through hearing and understanding him. Rather, we can simply experience the love that surpasses knowledge (Ephesians 3) and is deep in our hearts as God draws us deeper into relationship with him.

We all hear and respond to God in different ways that can be different at different times. Quite often God speaks to me through a thought which then becomes a visual image, which I can imagine in the same way I might imagine what my favourite food looks like. God has also spoken to me though through a feeling in my skin, a deep sense of peace, or a particular phrase or passage in the Bible. There isn't one right way for us to hear and respond to God.

Practically, this looks like providing as many different opportunities as possible through which individuals can encounter God through the power of his Holy Spirit. We can do this through typical prayer ministry models, such as opening our hands, having others put a hand on our shoulder, and asking God to speak to us through the power of his Spirit. We might then hear God's voice, see a picture in our mind's eye, think something he's speaking, feel something in our skin, or have a deep sense of knowing. But we can also pray in lots of different ways. If we are praying with children and young people or adults with significant learning disabilities we could knock down a tower and through this action pray that God enables us to be bold. We could blow bubbles and they could be the very prayer that we are creating, then we could pop them and say thank you to God for different things. We could lie under a parachute and spend time feeling the breeze and asking God to breathe over us with his Spirit. We could hold and shape clay as a way of expressing how we're feeling and listening to God's response to us. We could sit wrapped up in a blanket to experience God's protection and love surrounding us. We could go on a walk and, as we breathe in that incredible leafy smell of being in the countryside, ask God to speak to the depths of our being about the freedom he gives us and the wide-open space he draws us into through his salvation. The possibilities are endless. There are so many different ways that we can listen to God and respond to his voice in our lives.

One children's pastor contacted me recently about how we support children with additional needs to experience and know (in their hearts) God's voice speaking to them. A young boy called Sam had been at the New Wine United gatherings and had heard about how we can 'hang out' with God. Sam has a diagnosis of autism and because of this finds it difficult not to take things literally. In his mind 'hanging out' with individuals involves being able to see them and talk to them physically. He told his mum that he had been waiting for over a year for God to answer his question, 'God, what are you doing today?' As Sam hadn't physically heard an *auditory* response from God, he didn't think God was talking to him. This was impacting Sam's ability to be able to participate in church and he was starting to refuse to go along to kid's ministry with his peers. Chatting with the children's pastor about how she had spoken to Sam and his family, we created a downloadable resource which is available at https://www.new-wine.org/sites/default/files/resources/download//2017//12/childrens_poster.pdf). It looks at all the different ways God can speak to us and that we can hear his voice. As individuals with autism often take things very literally, we need to be careful about how we use language to explain what it's like to hear and recognise God's voice. Explaining that God can often speak through a thought that pops into our head or something in our imagination (such as when we close our eyes and think what our favourite car looks like) can often be helpful.

At the United gatherings all the venues explore different ways that we can enable children, young people and adults to experience a deeper connection and relationship with God through the power of the Holy Spirit. One venue called Rock Solid for 8-9 year olds often has a 'shack at the back'. This is a prayer space that children can access at any point during the session to be prayed for and to experience different ways of God speaking to them.

This idea is borrowed from a church I was a part of. Here we created a cupboard with doors that opened up and a roof that pulled out to create a quick fold-away 'shack at the back'. It can also be a space for inclusion, the idea being that all children in the group can use the 'shack at the back' as a space to retreat to if everything's too much, but also to participate and hear what God is saying to them. This is a space where children can find something to hold in their hands if they need it, to move around, or to bounce on a gym ball if it's helpful, and to have an adult's support. This all enables each child to participate in the session and hear what God is saying to them.

So what about adults? How can we create multisensory opportunities and ways to pray that don't appear to be childish and enable everyone to participate? I think what Pete Greig and the 24/7 movement have done with prayer rooms is an incredible example of this. Having multisensory ways in which individuals of all ages can engage in prayer and hear and respond to God's voice is amazing. We can think about how this can be translated to the bigger setting of corporate prayer. I find that churches often do this at Easter; they might place a nail at the cross, put a stone in a bucket, plant a seed etc. However, we could do this throughout the year, perhaps with individuals holding a specific object. Perhaps a section of church could be set-up with paint, clay and other materials that could help people respond to what God is saying. One of the things that a church I've been a part of has done is to enable individuals to paint and respond to God through creating a canvas or piece of art during the service.

Think about how you prefer to hear God's voice. Do you connect with him most when you read his word? When you're out in creation? When you feel his presence on your skin? When you hear him speak in a different way? We can choose to enable everyone to engage with that deeper knowing of God's love for us through creating multisensory opportunities that enable everyone to engage.

Chapter 5: Smell and Remember
Understanding Our Olfactory Sense

'Six days before the Passover, Jesus therefore came to Bethany, where Lazarus was, whom Jesus had raised from the dead. So they gave a dinner for him there. Martha served, and Lazarus was one of those reclining with him at the table. Mary therefore took a pound of expensive ointment made from pure nard, and anointed the feet of Jesus and wiped his feet with her hair. The house was filled with the fragrance of the perfume. But Judas Iscariot, one of his disciples (he who was about to betray him), said, "Why was this ointment not sold for three hundred denarii and given to the poor?" He said this not because he cared about the poor, but because he was a thief, and having charge of the moneybag he used to help himself to what was put into it. Jesus said, "Leave her alone, so that she may keep it for the day of my burial. For the poor you always have with you, but you do not always have me."*
(John 12: 1-8)

Our sense of smell is an interesting one. It's called our *olfactory* sense and it is received through receptors in our nose. We process the smells around us, which support our sense of taste and enable us to respond to danger (such as with the smell of smoke or gas) or pleasure (such as the smell of chocolate).

Close your eyes for a moment and see if you can think of an early memory of a time where you felt happy or excited. What did it smell like? I remember being in ballet shows and this memory always conjures up the smell of hairspray and make-up. If I smell hairspray or make-up now, I'm often transported back to that feeling of excitement and anticipation of being in a ballet show as a child. Our olfactory system is closely linked to our limbic system. One of the things the limbic system does is help us to process our memories and emotions. That's why sometimes a certain smell can trigger a particular memory. I wonder how many of you, when you smell a particular perfume are reminded of a specific individual? There is a link between our sense of smell and our memory.

I love the way that our brains are such complex neurological systems and yet provide us with so many different ways of connecting with God and being reminded of his presence. The Bible describes an abundance of strong smells and the way in which the disciples responded to them. I wonder if this is because of the link between smell and memory?

In the Old Testament we read that as part of their worship the Jews would offer sacrifices to God which were a *pleasing aroma* to him. Perhaps that pleasing aroma also enabled individuals to recall God's grace and love for them as his chosen people.

In the passage at the start of this chapter, towards the end of Jesus' life, we see Mary anoint Jesus' feet with perfume. We read that *'the house was filled with the fragrance of the perfume'*. The smell of the perfume and the act of Mary anointing Jesus' feet was a preparation for his death and resurrection. Since the smell 'filled' the house, it probably didn't dissipate very quickly. The connection between that fragrant smell and the sacrifice that Jesus made in dying on the cross was probably one that stuck powerfully in the disciples' minds. It would have become a powerful reminder of what Jesus faced in order to give everyone the opportunity for redemption.

Another strong smell which we see come up time and again in the Bible is the smell of fish. I'm not a massive fan of eating fish and I'm definitely not a fan of the smell! But I wonder how much God used this strong smell as a means of reminding his people of his provision? Jesus regularly encounters his disciples when fishing. In the feeding of the 4,000 and the 5,000 I expect the multiplication of so much fish must have created a distinct smell. Within the brains of all the individuals there, it is likely that a link would have been created between the incredible sense of elation and amazement at Jesus' provision for them, and the smell of the fish. Perhaps each time those people ate fish afterwards, they were reminded of God's incredible provision and love for them.

God may or may not have spoken to you through your sense of smell already. As we become more aware of the different ways that we process the world around us through our bodies, we can be aware of the potential of smell – the connection between what we smell and what we feel and remember. Are there ways in which you can create smells that connect with the topic you're exploring in your teaching? Perhaps you could pierce a tin of tuna and use the smell of fish? Or use a sycamore scented candle when speaking about the tree that Zaccheus climbed. Perhaps, if you're near the beach when there's a storm you could reflect on the distinct smell of a stormy sea and the peace that Jesus brings when he stills the storm.

One Sunday in the church I attend, in order to illustrate the way that we carry the aroma of Christ (2 Corinthians 2:15) our vicar planted a few people with perfume sprayed on their hands. Without knowing, we all shook lots of people's hands and by the time everyone sat down most people had the smell of the perfume on their hands. We are carriers of the fragrance of Jesus. Just as the fire of God's kingdom spreads as we light those sparks, we can choose to step out by carrying his fragrance and his presence with us wherever we go. As people smell the distinct fragrance of Christ they are more likely to be able to experience, feel and remember the incredible love he gives which surpasses our head knowledge.

A small note about our sense of smell: some individuals can be hypersensitive to smells and find it difficult to process them. With all of our senses we all have different preferences and experiences related to them which we find harder or easier to process and utilise in the way that we understand the world. For individuals who are hypersensitive to smell, this can be so overwhelming that the smell of a particular room or a particular person's perfume can prevent an individual from going near the source of that smell. This is relatively rare and quite difficult to address directly. However, one strategy that worked well with a child who refused to go into the school tech room because of its smell was to put flavoured Vaseline on her nose each tech lesson. This meant that the girl was able to go into her class and smell the Vaseline, rather than the smell of the room and could therefore participate fully.

How do you respond to smell? Perhaps there are certain smells mentioned in Bible passages you're teaching which you could replicate and use to enable individuals to connect more easily with what God is saying.

Chapter 6: Taste and See the Lord is Good
Understanding Our Gustatory Sense

'Taste and see that the Lord is good; blessed is the one who takes refuge in him.'
(Psalm 34:8)

I wonder if this is something you've reflected on before? *Taste and see that the Lord is good.* We can see God is good through the very way that we taste and experience the food we consume. As we reflected in the previous chapter, our memory is closely linked to our sense of smell, which is also closely linked to our sense of taste. The individuals at the feeding of the 5,000 may have been reminded of Jesus' incredible provision each time they smelt and ate fish. They had tasted and seen that God was good and quite possibly this enabled them to remember his goodness. Our sense of taste (*gustatory* sense) is experienced via taste receptors in our mouth. These receptors send signals to our brain about the properties of food. Depending on our preferences, we then process and react to what we taste in a positive or negative way.

Food is essential to our bodies and vital for us to be able to flourish and thrive. God has created us with the need to be able to process nutrients from our food in order to survive. Food, and the taste of food, is an essential part of our lives. Some individuals I've encountered aren't able to eat through their mouth because they have difficulty with chewing and swallowing. Instead, they will often have a nasal gastric tube (a tube from their nose to their stomach) or a PEG (Percutaneous endoscopic gastrostomy – a tube which is attached to the outside of their tummy and goes through to their stomach). These individuals, even though they cannot eat food using their mouths, can sometimes still have a small taste on their lips to enable the experience of taste. (Please don't ever do this without checking and being shown how by caregivers!) Often the taste of food is very motivating, and is a good, satisfying experience. When we eat something we like, it feels good. God can use this sense to enable us to connect with the incredible way he's made us and provides for us.

In my flat we have a jug which has the verse 'taste and see the Lord is good' on it. It's often filled with a sticky toffee sauce or cream at pudding time. As we share the jug around the table and taste the delicious food, it's an unspoken reminder of God's provision and goodness. Mealtimes are often a great place for sharing and being community. Being around a table seems to be a significant place for conversation with others. I can recall several deep conversations over a meal with friends in which people have spoken into my life and I have seen more of what God wants to say to me. We see this throughout Jesus' life. He often gathered around a table with his disciples, and with tax collectors, Pharisees and other individuals he wasn't expected to be with.

Being around a table and eating food is not always easy for everyone. We know that many individuals with mental health needs have a difficult relationship with food which impacts their ability to eat in front of others, or to taste and see God's goodness through eating. We can be careful about the way in which we organise meals for events, so that they are not always based around food. If we give people the opportunity to serve themselves, or to have a choice within a meal, it can be easier for some individuals to cope. If you are aware of someone who has difficulty with eating there is support available from charities such as Taste Life UK. Some individuals also have difficulties with eating because of physical needs or because of sensory processing difficulties. I have met and worked with several children who find the texture and taste of many foods difficult to deal with (because of hypersensitivity to touch and taste) and therefore they have a very restricted diet.

One little boy I worked with, Alfie, had a very restricted diet and would not eat several foods. As an occupational therapist part of my role can be to help children expand their diet. For Alfie this involved a range of activities in therapy sessions that helped him to increase his awareness of his mouth, so that he could more easily process what he was tasting. That took the pressure off exploring foods so that this process felt safe.

When we help children explore different foods we draw upon the understanding that there are several different stages to tasting and then eating something. We first have to be comfortable in the same room as a certain food, then being near the food, touching the food, putting the food near our mouths, touching it with our lips, holding it in our lips, holding it in our mouths and spitting it out, biting it and spitting it out, and finally chewing it and spitting out, before eating a very small amount. Alfie was at the point where he could be in the same room, but would often gag or cry if he had to touch a food he did not like, such as cheese, chicken or vegetables. In his first session, Alfie tried biting a cherry tomato to see what it was like and had such a negative reaction to it that he was sick all over the table. Although it was not the reaction we were hoping for, we calmly moved onto the next foods (enabling Alfie to then eat something he felt safe with) because we wanted him to know that it was okay to try things.

Over the course of six months Alfie and I played lots of games where we kissed different foods, played the 'no hands' game and had competitions to see who could hold them in their mouths with no hands for the longest. We fed lots of food to 'monster' (a plastic monster in the middle of the table who could eat food up), and talked about how we chew food to eat it. Gradually, Alfie became more comfortable with exploring foods he did not like, to the point where he started to be able to eat some of those foods as part of meals at home. Alfie is now able to eat carrots and green beans, both of which he was unable to put in his mouth before we started.

For Alfie, even though it was a long process, the opportunity to learn to eat a slightly broader range of foods has meant he now can receive more of the nutrients he needs in his diet, and he has a greater ability to participate in meals with his family. Alfie has learnt that it is safe to try tasting different things and to practise doing so in order to grow and expand his diet.

This could be an illustration of the way that we enable others to explore, learn and grow in their faith. When we encounter individuals with additional needs, and when we stick strongly to our own preferences, it can be difficult for everyone to have the opportunity to experience the fullness that God has for them. Just like Alfie's restricted diet prevented him from being able to get all the nutrients he needed in his food, and to be able to participate in meals with his family, if we only do things in one specific way, this may restrict the opportunity for everyone to participate in church family. Although creating a more accessible culture can be a long process and take lots of steps (just like it did helping Alfie to explore new foods) it is such a rewarding process and can enable the whole church family to learn so much.

One example of this is in a church where it took several meetings and the perseverance of the parent of a child with additional needs to put accessibility on the church's agenda. However, after continuing to try and gain the support and wisdom of others, the church community slowly started to understand. The church then asked individuals with expertise to give training and this led to the whole church family being more readily able to respond to and meet the needs of individuals who came along.

Part of creating greater accessibility for everyone within church is about giving more *multisensory* opportunities for everyone to engage in. Taste is one sense which can be used as part of this. We can think about different ways we could use our sense of taste to help people understand and connect with what Jesus is saying. We could all eat honey or caramel sweets as we reflect on *'[God's] word being like honey to our lips'* (Psalm 119:103). We could eat fish and bread as we remember Jesus' miraculous provision for the 4,000 and the 5,000 on the mountainside. Perhaps we may then start to create a memory, because the connection in our brains between smell, taste and memory will enable us to recall God's provision in our lives when we eat fish or bread. I have heard of some kids ministries where all the children have made bread as part of thinking about the kingdom of God spreading like yeast (Matthew 13:33). What a multisensory way to connect with God's call on us to be a part of expanding his kingdom!

Jesus also used taste to enable understanding as part of his teaching. God is a multisensory God and therefore enables us to understand what he's saying and doing through all of the senses he's given us. We see one example right at the start of Jesus' ministry where he miraculously makes something really tasty. In John 2 Jesus turns water into wine. We see the Master of the feast say to the bridegroom, *'Everyone serves the good wine first, and when people have drunk freely, then the poor wine. But you have kept the good wine until now.'* We read that after this event Jesus' disciples believed in him. They had learnt something through their sense of taste which demonstrated Jesus' miraculous power.

Taste is probably a sense that you already use quite a lot in your church services, but you could also perhaps use a bit more. The opportunity to have a cup of tea or coffee and perhaps a biscuit, some cake or a piece of fruit when you come into church is a great way to give people something they can connect over. For an adult who is feeling they are on the edge of the group, having something they can do (such as go and get a drink) can often help them to feel more welcome. Also enabling adults to serve on a hospitality team can be something that really helps people feel a part of church community. This can sometimes be an area where adults with additional needs really enjoy serving. Certainly we have found this at New Wine's United gatherings where we support several individuals to work on the café teams.

There are so many individuals who I've met over the tea and coffee station at church. Next time you go and get a tea or coffee, or are serving it, take time to say 'hi' to the person you meet. If you don't know it, ask their name, and ask how their week has been. Take time to connect. God is a God of connection. He longs for us to be in relationship with him and to live in community with each other. We can start to create community through a simple 'hello, how are you?'

At my local church in King's Cross another way in which we use our sense of taste is in the break in our service (we'll talk about the break a bit later in Chapter 9). When the collection basket is passed around. a basket of Maoams is also passed around. The great thing about this is that everyone has the opportunity to take one and to chew while they're listening to the talk. Again we'll look at why chewing is so great in Chapter 9, but having chewy or crunchy snacks can really help us to feel regulated and ready to listen. This is a great strategy that enables everyone to concentrate more easily.

We also use this within kids ministry. When we tell a story to our 1-5s on a Sunday morning we give them the opportunity to have a drink and a bread stick. This helps them to focus on the story and enables them to keep their attention while they listen.

Thinking about different snacks we can use to help change people's level of regulation is a part of therapy practice. I was on a course where an experienced occupational therapist training on attachment told the story of a child in foster care who had a very difficult relationship with his birth parents but continued to have arranged contact time. The contact time with the birth mum was always difficult and ended up with aggression and upset on both sides. The occupational therapist decided to try and help calm the situation by using a snack to help regulate everyone. Each individual in the meeting was given a Boost bar (chewy, crunchy chocolate) and they found that the contact time went much smoother than it ever had before. What we eat and the properties of what we eat can have a big impact on how we feel. Although we won't know everyone's preferences, it is something we can think about in the activities we run.

We know that certain tastes and foods will be calming and certain tastes and foods will be alerting. This will differ according to the person, but often a tangy or spicy taste like lemon or chilli will be alerting and something like chocolate or vanilla will be calming. We also know that chewy and crunchy snacks (like the Maoams or raw carrot or apple) will help us to get to a 'just right' level where we can focus on what we're doing. This week why don't you try something different with food? Try introducing a snack. Use something crunchy or chewy like bread sticks, carrot or Maoams and see if it helps to change something in the room.

Chapter 7: Touch That Transforms
Understanding Our Tactile Sense

'As Jesus was on his way, the crowds almost crushed him. And
a woman was there who had been subject to bleeding for twelve
years, but no one could heal her. She came up behind him and
touched the edge of his cloak, and immediately her bleeding
stopped. "Who touched me?" Jesus asked. When they all denied
it, Peter said, "Master, the people are crowding and pressing
against you." But Jesus said, "Someone touched me; I know that
power has gone out from me." Then the woman, seeing that she
could not go unnoticed, came trembling and fell at his feet. In
the presence of all the people, she told why she had touched him
and how she had been instantly healed. Then he said to her,
"Daughter, your faith has healed you. Go in peace."
(Luke 8:42-48)

Touch is powerful. Research studies have shown that if we do
not receive touch it has significantly damaging effects on our
health, development and wellbeing (Ardiel & Rankin 2010[1]).
Researcher Dr Paul Zak suggested in his TED talk in 2011 that

1. Ardiel, E.L, Ranking, C.H. (2010) The importance of touch development.
Paediatrics and Child Health, March: 153-156.

in order to keep this level of wellbeing everyone would benefit from at least 8 hugs a day!

In the opening passage in Luke 8 we see that Jesus' touch transforms. The woman touches his cloak and through that touch is healed. Her life is transformed. She goes from being a woman who is stuck in her house, shunned by her community, to someone who can *go in peace* and be a part of the community she has been estranged from. Jesus' healing enables her to have a new fullness of life, an opportunity to know his love and acceptance as a *daughter* of God, but also to be able to be known and valued within the society where she lives.

You are probably familiar with Mother Theresa who founded the Missionaries of Charity and, alongside others, served vulnerable individuals in India. Mother Theresa famously stated that the congregation would care for 'the hungry, the naked, the homeless, the crippled, the blind, the lepers, all those people who feel unwanted, unloved, uncared for throughout society, people that have become a burden to the society and are shunned by everyone.' She chose to see individuals with value; to touch individuals, such as those with leprosy, who were shunned by their communities. She knew that she was loved and accepted by God and she chose to practically enable others to know that love. She made a choice that transformed many lives.

Mother Theresa appears to have realised something which we see so clearly in Jesus' life. On several occasions Jesus chose to touch and relate to individuals who he was expected *not* to interact with. He touched people with leprosy (Matthew 7). He allowed a women to anoint his feet and wipe them with her hair (Luke 7). He washed the disciples feet (John 13).

Each time Jesus enabled touch to happen he was challenging societal norms. Jesus' touch not only transformed the lives of the individuals he touched, but spoke beyond the individual to his culture. Jesus' touch demonstrates that God's love reaches to individuals who are viewed unclean or unimportant. Individuals with leprosy would have been seen as unclean and were forced to live apart from their families and community. Jesus' touch spoke of value and provided the opportunity for belonging. Jesus acted outside of cultural expectations to challenge the status quo.

I wonder how often we choose to do something which is outside of our cultural expectations or norms? Touch is a tricky subject and in order to keep everyone safe in church we need to be very careful with where, when and how we touch. Hopefully this is something we already do well in our churches (only ever placing hands on someone's shoulder or an appropriate part of their body after asking them, and only giving hugs in public places). When we put a hand on someone's shoulder in ministry we are using touch in a positive manner – our touch enables the individual to know that we're there, standing with them, contending for them that they might know more of the Holy Spirit in their life.

Counter cultural touch within a church community might be using touch as a part of *multisensory* learning and teaching. Enabling individuals to feel and touch different objects or textures can enable them to engage and learn more easily.

There are so many ways we can use touch as part of multisensory teaching within church settings. There are lots of possibilities for giving individuals something to touch and feel as part of engaging with teaching or a story. Holding a nail to think about the crucifixion, holding some cloth to think about the empty grave and left-behind grave clothes at the resurrection, being wrapped in a soft blanket when thinking about Jesus' love and protection are all examples. I still remember services where I had the opportunity to hold a stone and put it at the foot of the cross. It is such a powerful reminder of the weight of our sin and the freedom of being able to come before Jesus and lay it at his feet. Recently in Kid's church, we walked through flour to think about the dirty, sandy feet the disciples would have had before Jesus washed them. Practically, feeling the story as well as hearing about it enables us to engage at a deeper level.

When Jesus touched and healed the man with leprosy he restored his sense of touch and his ability to feel and discriminate different touches (when you have leprosy your touch receptors feel numb and therefore you cannot process touch or feel if you're in pain). Jesus not only restored the man's *tactile* sense, he enabled him to be a part of his community again. Not only would this have meant being able to interact with friends and family, but also being able to have a job and gain wellbeing and satisfaction from participating in society. As an occupational therapist I can see how transforming this touch from Jesus would have been for this person. Not only did he then have the opportunity to feel the world around him, to avoid injury and complete tasks requiring dexterity, he also had the opportunity for occupation; for doing something meaningful with his life. This is so important (and well researched). We know that meaningful occupation has a significantly positive impact upon health and wellbeing.

So how is touch experienced? We experience touch through receptors in our skin. These receptors tell us about the different properties of touch. Receptors near the top of our skin (such as the hairs on the surface) tell us about light, tickly touch – this is often alerting and can feel a bit uncomfortable, for example, if something brushes past us when we don't expect it. We also have receptors deep within the layers of our skin. These receptors process what we call *deep pressure* touch. We know that deep pressure touch is calming and helps us to feel secure.

Let me tell you a story about some young twins, Libby and Ellie. Both Libby and Ellie absolutely love exploring. They love playing outside and being able to climb and run and jump. When they're at home they tend to get out lots of toys at once and enjoy feeling and playing with everything. They both absolutely love wildlife and exploring in the garden. They like to look at the worms, they like to climb trees and jump off rocks.

One day Libby and Ellie wanted to play in the garden and asked their Mummy if it was okay. Their Mummy told them they needed to put on their wellies first, so that their feet didn't get wet as they explored. Libby quickly ran to the door, her Mummy helped her to put her wellies on and she went out into the garden exploring.

Ellie was different. Ellie got to the door and her Mummy came to help her with her wellies. As Ellie's Mum touched Ellie's foot with her wellie Ellie screamed, 'Ow!' She burst into tears and started to kick her feet, refusing to put her wellies on, even though she wanted to go into the garden. Ellie's Mummy scooped Ellie up and gave her a big hug, she tucked her socks into her trousers, held her foot and wellie firmly and Ellie let her put them on. Ellie was then able to go outside and play with Libby, soon enjoying the opportunity to explore with her sister.

So what happened for Ellie? Instead of processing the touch and understanding it, Ellie had interpreted the touch as painful. Ellie's Mum was able to use *deep pressure* touch to enable Ellie to feel calm and process the sensation of putting her wellies on in order to go out and play.

Every individual has two neurological pathways, which send messages from our skin to our brain, in order to process touch. The first touch pathway, which we develop in the womb, is our *protective pathway* which tells us about pain and temperature. The second touch pathway is our *discriminative pathway* which tells us about the properties and textures of what we feel. If, like Ellie, we find it difficult to process touch, we may have a tendency to use our protective rather than discriminative touch pathway. This means we can perceive a touch which does not actually hurt us as painful. We can help to reduce this through the use of *deep pressure* touch and *proprioception* (which we'll talk about in Chapter 9).

Individual's with Autism quite commonly display a hypersensitivity to touch (sometimes known as tactile defensiveness). Although touch sensitivity is common for individuals with autism, other individuals may find touch difficult too. It is important that we are aware of this. Many individuals will tell you or make it clear as to their preference for touch, or no touch, but not everyone will. We could decide to check before we give a hug or a handshake, or we could check with individuals we know might find touch difficult. If we use touch, such as a hand on the shoulder for praying, or encouraging a child to move across a room, we can think about the amount of pressure we use. Neurologically, deep pressure touch is easier to process. Therefore, a whole hand, firmly placed, can help individuals who have tactile sensitivities.

It is important to note that sometimes individuals who have experienced abuse, or have attachment disorders, may find touch really difficult, particularly from individuals who are unfamiliar to them. If you are notified about an individual who has had this kind of experience, it might be good to have a conversation about touch and what helps the individual feel most safe.

Why is touch so important? Touch is one of the most foundational senses, one of the first to develop when we're a baby in the womb. When we are little we learn to process a lot of the world around us through our sense of touch. We experience touch in the process of being cared for – of being held, dressed, fed, changed, bathed. We learn to understand toys and experience objects through feeling with our mouths – you'll often see babies putting first their hands (and then everything they come across!) into their mouths. Our mouths are one of the most sensitive parts of our body and the sensory system through which we process a lot. We will often subconsciously put our hand to our chin or our mouth if we're finding it difficult to concentrate. This is a regulating sensation. Because our mouth is more sensitive to touch, it helps us to feel calmer and more regulated if we receive touch around our mouths. This is why sometimes eating particular things can help us concentrate. As our mouth is sensitive to sensory stimuli, like chewing gum or sucking a boiled sweet, we can help achieve a greater sense of regulation in our bodies.

Some individuals will seek out touch more than others. You may or may not be familiar with the five love languages[2] but touch is one of the ways that some individuals prefer to give and receive love. Although touch is important for social and emotional wellbeing for all of us, it may be even more so for individuals for whom touch is their primary love language. Whilst being aware of individuals who do not like touch, we can also be aware of individuals who love touch and this enables them to thrive.

A story from the local church of an adult with Down's Syndrome shows the importance of her being able to touch and experience touch as a part of her church family. Bella's mum and dad did an Alpha course and had the opportunity to experience the love of Jesus for themselves and to know the love and value he has for every individual. Bella has quite significant additional needs – she does not have verbal language and often chooses to communicate through making noises, touching others and indicating her needs through non-verbal communication. Bella lives in the community with support, but comes along to church with her parents each week.

Through trying church out, Bella's parents found that she benefitted most from the routine and predictability of the traditional communion service rather than the informal worship service. Bella absolutely loves it. She loves singing and joins in enthusiastically. She normally needs several trips to the toilet each service and will often stroke and touch the people around her, seemingly randomly. The church community have accepted Bella with open arms. The congregation is mainly

2. Chapman, G (2015) The 5 Love Languages Paperback, Moody Press.

made up of older adults and they welcome and love Bella each week. They greet her as she wanders past them on her way to the toilet and they chat with her before and after services.

Bella is an individual who has found love and acceptance within her church community. Her joy and love of touch no doubt brings joy and opportunity for connection and interaction for some of the older adults who may be living alone and may not receive this during the rest of the week. Bella's parents know that Bella is loved, accepted and has something to offer within God's kingdom, just as they do. Bella's need for touch and her love of this isn't rejected by the church community, but is welcomed. We see in the Bible that Jesus touched and transformed lives. This may also be true for Bella – her touch has the possibility of transforming others; of enabling them to know and experience the love that Jesus has for them.

I know that for me (with touch as one of my love languages) there have been times when someone coming over and hugging me has been significant, has transformed my day and reminded me that I belong.

Touch is so foundational that the more multisensory approaches which involve touch we use, the more individuals are able to learn. We see this within occupational therapy practice. Children who have the opportunity to learn shape and letter formation in different textures, such as sand, shaving foam, corn flour and water, have much more ability to learn because they not only *see* the shape, they *feel* it as well.

We all have the ability to use this sense God had given us, that has such a big impact upon our health and wellbeing, to see Jesus transform peoples lives. It is complicated and there isn't a one size fits all approach, but the more aware we are of the transforming power of touch the more we can understand the impact it has upon our lives.

Over the next few weeks, as you prepare to teach others, perhaps think about what something might feel like to touch. How could you use touch to enable others to connect to the story? How could you use *deep pressure* touch to help someone to more readily know they are welcome and accepted?

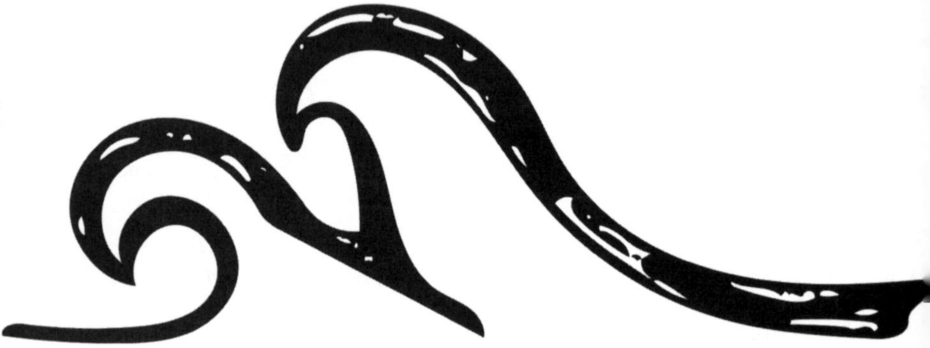

Chapter 8: Gaining Balance
Understanding Our Vestibular Sense

'That day when evening came, he said to his disciples, "Let us go over to the other side." Leaving the crowd behind, they took him along, just as he was, in the boat. There were also other boats with him. A furious squall came up, and the waves broke over the boat, so that it was nearly swamped. Jesus was in the stern, sleeping on a cushion. The disciples woke him and said to him, "Teacher, don't you care if we drown?" He got up, rebuked the wind and said to the waves, "Quiet! Be still!" Then the wind died down and it was completely calm. He said to his disciples, "Why are you so afraid? Do you still have no faith?" They were terrified and asked each other, "Who is this? Even the wind and the waves obey him!"
(Mark 4:35-41)

Losing our balance can be an embarrassing thing. When I was probably thirteen or so I went to a youth group which was a mixture of a small number of youth from church and a very large number of youth from the local secondary school across the road. I was at that awkward stage where fitting in felt really important and it was hard to know what was the 'right' thing to do in every situation. One Friday night, I went to the hall downstairs with a couple of friends to join in with whatever was happening there. Some boys were kicking a giant tennis ball around and the ball rolled over to me. I pride myself on being able to kick a football (having three younger brothers, a penalty shoot-out was not an uncommon game in our house). However, on this occasion I experienced embarrassment rather than pride! As the ball rolled towards me, I stepped back to take a big kick to launch it back, but instead of kicking the ball, I managed to swing my leg so hard that I put myself off balance. I ended up launching myself flat on my back on the floor, slightly dazed by the momentum I'd managed to achieve! I'd like to blame it on the quality of the giant tennis ball, or the spin of the kick which headed towards me, but the reality is I just lost my balance.

In that moment, not only did I physically lose my balance, I also felt like I'd lost my balance in the situation I was in. I felt shame and embarrassment because something I'd done was outside of what was 'right' and normal when at youth group. It was a ground-swallow-me-up kind of moment and I didn't know where to look or what to do. No doubt I went bright red, just to enhance my sense of shame. It was my friends who helped me to physically and metaphorically regain my balance. They laughed with me, we chose to go back upstairs to do something different, and the moment was forgotten.

There are times in life when we need to be able to hold our head upright and know the direction we're going in. Our *vestibular* sense – our sense of balance – tells us how fast we're moving and the direction we're moving in. God has given us this incredible sense, and as well as physically enabling us to gain our balance, there are times in which he can metaphorically enable us to regain our sense of direction.

In the Bible there are several examples of God enabling people to gain their balance. There are times where individuals feel their life is out of kilter and God reaches in and helps to right them, giving them a sense of who they are and the direction they are heading in.

God spoke clearly to Jonah, even though he initially didn't want to listen, drew him out of the whale (which would have definitely been an intense vestibular experience!) and set him on the shore. God constantly enables people who are walking in the wrong direction to turn around and go the way he is calling them. Jesus often helped his disciples regain their 'balance'. One example is in the passage at the start of this chapter where the disciples were in the middle of a storm. With their vestibular and balance systems going haywire, the disciples couldn't help but panic. Jesus is fully human, so his body would also have been subject to the same intense vestibular input as the disciples, yet he taught the disciples the peace he brings, and the trust they could have in God, through the act of sleeping through the storm. Jesus' sense of calm, and his command to the waves to 'be still', may have impacted the disciples more than the act of the storm ceasing. Following an intense movement experience that was probably making them feel sick, the stillness would have brought instant relief and peace. On top of that, Jesus was showing them that he was in control. He was there with them, keeping them going in the right direction, even when they were afraid.

If you are in the initial stages of setting up additional needs ministry, perhaps the amount of need that has appeared in your church, or that God has opened your eyes to see, is making you feel off balance. Perhaps you feel like the disciples in this passage, surrounded by waves. Maybe you have a child who comes along to kids ministry and runs around and doesn't sit and listen each week. Maybe you have an adult with a learning disability who has started coming along to your community, but they have some behavioural issues which are difficult to handle. Maybe you're on track in creating accessible church ministry, but because you're so good it's drawn in a number of other families and the volume of need feels difficult to manage. Or perhaps everything is going well and you do not remotely feel like you're in a storm. Whichever place you're in, I think there's value in reflecting on this passage and taking time to 'be still'. To think about the fact that Jesus had so much peace that he was able to sleep in a storm.

We know that even in the face of such extreme vestibular input, Jesus can still the waves. Psalm 46:10 says, 'Be still and know that I am God', which reminds us of the deep heart knowledge that we can have when we stop still. This is such an incredible promise. For me, personally, there have been so many times in life when I've realised I have been rushing from one thing to another and I couldn't remember the last time I'd stopped to be still. Whether we're facing an extreme storm or just the everyday bombardment of movement activity, there are times with Jesus that we can 'be still'.

Why not try it now? Stop reading for a minute, take two minutes to be still. Two minutes to stop moving, to rest your vestibular sense; to recalibrate and know which way you're heading with Jesus.

I set up additional needs ministry within a local, week-long holiday club that gave a huge number of non-church children the opportunity to hear about Jesus. Lighthouse is now a national endeavour, running holiday clubs across the country with around 5,000 children and 3,000 volunteers (www. lighthousecentral.org). The reason I set up the additional needs ministry within my local lighthouse was that I had been to the New Wine summer event as a young helper and seen the importance of inclusion, and the way that it worked within the venues there. I decided that it was important to have the same provision at the holiday club I was involved in at my local church at home. Yet, when I first set it up, it felt a bit like being in the middle of that storm. Although I had a heart and a desire to see God move, and to provide and support children who I knew needed a bit more help to join in, I was young and inexperienced. I was still at school and apart from my experience of supporting a handful of children with additional needs, I did not have any professional training. With the incredible backing of the Lighthouse leadership team and my local church, I set up systems to find out the children's needs, to communicate with their group leaders, and to make sure they received the support they needed. I rang lots of my friends asking them to volunteer and help me (as a teenager, thankfully I had lots of friends who were on school holidays!) It generally went smoothly and we saw an incredible number of children with additional needs supported to participate in everything that was happening.

Despite this, there were a few moments where things went a bit awry and the storm felt undeniably present. We had a couple of children who needed one-on-one support and and a friend and I were supporting two children in the same group, helping them move around site and participate in activities. What we hadn't anticipated was that one of the children loved to sit down and refused to move, while the other child loved to run away! There was a moment where I found myself in a courtyard with my friend on one side, encouraging one child to move, and myself running across the other side to support the other child and trying to stop them completely disappearing from view. In the end it was all okay and we were able to engage the children and encourage them to participate and move back to their groups, but in the moment the situation felt shaky. As we grew the team across the years we gained more experience, more professional volunteers, and more training, all of which helped us to see more children and their families included. The moments that felt like being in a storm were part of the learning that enabled lighthouse to be as accessible as it is now (from the initial set up in the one lighthouse, *The Space* now runs inclusion across each local lighthouse). Through those times, remembering the vision and prayerfully considering what we were doing and how we were doing it helped us to regain our balance and get back on the right track.

It is okay to feel like things are a bit out of control. Part of working with children, young people and adults with additional needs is that, often, unpredictable things happen. Countless encounters I have had in my work with children and adults with additional needs have been challenging and at times scary. I have had a young adult scream and shout in my face, a child with such bad nits that you could see them crawling on her forehead, a vulnerable adult disclose safeguarding concerns and ask that I didn't tell their parents, and more. Such situations can be difficult to handle but there was always a way forward. I spoke calmly to the young adult shouting at me and moved out of the way so he had space to vent his anger. I spoke carefully to the parent of the child with nits. I spoke to the

Safegaurding Officer and we worked out what we needed to tell the vulnerable adult's parents and how we could work with them as we did so. No matter how much preparation we put in, unexpected things will always happen. If we have a heart and a vision from God to see inclusion happen, we prepare to the best of our ability, and have wise people around us, we will always be able to learn from the unexpected things. God is with us, to enable us to regain our balance when things feel that they are shaken.

As our vestibular system tells us about how fast we're moving and the direction we're moving in, it becomes a compass to our body which enables us to move around and do all the things we do every day. God has given us this incredible physical system and on top of this he is our constant guide who leads us in the direction he is taking us. Jesus said to the disciples, '*When the Spirit of truth comes, he will guide you into all the truth, for he will not speak on his own authority, but whatever he hears he will speak, and he will declare to you the things that are to come.*' (John 16:13). The Holy Spirit is our guide. Whether we have an excellent vestibular system or not, the Spirit continues to be our guide, pointing us in the direction in which God wants us to go.

Some individuals have difficulties with their vestibular sense. With each of our senses it's possible to be under-responsive or hyper-responsive. For the vestibular sense this would impact us in different ways. If we are under-responsive to vestibular input it might take a lot of moving around, a lot of spinning or being upside down, for us to register the movement. An individual who is constantly spinning, lying upside-down or sitting backwards on chairs is often seeking more vestibular input so that they can register it. If we're over-responsive (or hyper-responsive) to vestibular input we might constantly feel sick or dizzy or be afraid of movement. An individual who is hyper-responsive may not be able to travel in a car without being sick. They may not be able to walk or climb up onto steps because their hypersensitivity means that what could be seen as a typical movement experience for most, feels terrifying for them.

For both types of individual, it's helpful to know the different ways we can help everyone to process vestibular input. Research and neuroscience would suggest that linear vestibular input is calming, while irregular, stop-start movement is alerting. This is because of the way our vestibular receptors are built into our brains – we have semi-circular canals which tell us about stop-start movements and a sponge like structure which tells us about linear movement. If we do an activity such as swinging in a blanket, bouncing on a trampoline, rolling over a gym ball, or jumping up and down on the spot, it's all within one plane of movement. This can help us to feel calm and regulated. All these movements are also quite intense. For an individual who finds it hard to register movement, this might help them to register and therefore stop seeking it and join in with the activity at hand.

This can be really helpful when we put it into practice. At Access (the accessible church adult provision at New Wine United summer gatherings) enabling Miah to roll forwards and backwards on a ball (and therefore receive lots of intense movement input) helped her to register the movement she was seeking and then sit, listen and participate in the story. Within kids inclusion as part of the Our Place team (the 0-18s accessible church provision at United) I remember a time when we had a little boy called Timmy with autism in Pebbles (the group for 3-4 year olds). Timmy found it difficult to sit still and was constantly running around the venue, spinning, jumping and picking up any toys he could find. For a lot of the session Timmy appeared to find it difficult to engage. As his one-to-one I was often trying to encourage him to look at what was happening, or to be in the same place as the other children in his group, quite often to no avail. Yet, as we got to know Timmy, and he got to know us throughout the week, we found ways in which he could participate and engage in what was going on. We found that if Timmy had the chance to swing in a blanket he would suddenly become much calmer and would participate in prayer by popping bubbles and listening to the song played over all the children. It was incredible to see the impact of movement for Timmy and the way it helped him to engage and connect with Jesus in that moment.

Another child that I supported within the Our Place venue (the venue which opens half way through the morning and provides specialist teaching for children who find it difficult to stay in the mainstream venue the whole time) really benefitted from intense movement. Abi needed the opportunity to sit and bounce on a gym ball the whole time whilst listening to the story. This meant that Abi could participate in discussion and was able to then recall and repeat back what she'd learnt to her parents when they picked her up at the end of the session.

It can be difficult to know where to start and there are times we can feel off balance. We can turn to God and help him to enable us to regain our direction and hold our heads high. We can also enable opportunities for linear movement in the things that we're doing, particularly if we are encountering individuals who seem to love to move. Often, after focusing on a bit of movement, we will then glimpse amazing moments of engagement and participation that we might have otherwise missed or not enabled. Over the next little while, why not try two things: take moments to *be still*, particularly when things are feeling overwhelming; and add in a linear movement activity to something you do, to see if it helps more individuals to participate.

Chapter 9: Made To Move
Understanding Our Proprioceptive Sense

'Now that same day two of them were going to a village called Emmaus, about seven miles from Jerusalem. They were talking with each other about everything that had happened. As they talked and discussed these things with each other, Jesus himself came up and walked along with them; but they were kept from recognising him. He asked them,

"What are you discussing together as you walk along?" They stood still, their faces downcast. One of them, named Cleopas, asked him, "Are you the only one visiting Jerusalem who does not know the things that have happened there in these days?"

"What things?" he asked. "About Jesus of Nazareth," they replied. "He was a prophet, powerful in word and deed before God and all the people. The chief priests and our rulers handed him over to be sentenced to death, and they crucified him; but we had hoped that he was the one who was going to redeem Israel. And what is more, it is the third day since all this took place. In addition, some of our women amazed us. They went to the tomb early this morning but didn't find his body. They came and told us that they had seen a vision of angels, who said he was alive. Then some of our companions went to the tomb and found it just as the women had said, but they did not see Jesus."

He said to them, "How foolish you are, and how slow to believe all that the prophets have spoken! Did not the Messiah have to suffer these things and then enter his glory?" And beginning with Moses and all the Prophets, he explained to them what was said in all the Scriptures concerning himself.

As they approached the village to which they were going, Jesus continued on as if he were going farther. But they urged him strongly, "Stay with us, for it is nearly evening; the day is almost over." So he went in to stay with them. When he was at the table with them, he took bread, gave thanks, broke it and began to give it to them. Then their eyes were opened and they recognised him, and he disappeared from their sight.

They asked each other, "Were not our hearts burning within us while he talked with us on the road and opened the Scriptures to us?" They got up and returned at once to Jerusalem. There they found the Eleven and those with them, assembled together and saying, "It is true! The Lord has risen and has appeared to Simon." Then the two told what had happened on the way, and how Jesus was recognised by them when he broke the bread.'

(Luke 24:13-33)

All the senses are important, but *proprioception* is my favourite sense. My friends and flatmates would all be able to tell you what it is and why it's important because I love to talk about it so much! As we move and go about our day to day activities, our *proprioceptive* sense tells us where our body is positioned in space. It is a subconscious awareness we get from receptors in our joints which send signals to our brain. Proprioception is my favourite sense because of its ability to help us to gain a *just right* level – to self-regulate and therefore more easily respond to and be a part of the world around us. Whereas all the other senses we've talked about (sight, sound, smell, taste, touch, balance) have different aspects which help us feel calm or alert, proprioception can help us feel *both* calm and alert. We get proprioceptive feedback to our brain through what we call 'heavy work' movement activities – activities that are always regulating. Whether we're feeling a bit drowsy and need waking up or whether we're running around and over excited, a *proprioceptive* activity will help us become more regulated.

If I close my eyes and put my hand in one position I can copy it with my other hand because I have a subconscious awareness of where my body is positioned. This is me being able to use my proprioceptive sense. This sense is really important to our coordinated movement and our ability to concentrate and attend to the activities we're taking part in. In the Bible we see lots of activities take place which would have given the disciples a sense of proprioception. I wonder if you've ever thought about the context of Jesus' encounters with his disciples? Often these are not static encounters where they sit and listen, but active encounters in which they have the opportunity to move.

We often see Jesus journeying with his disciples, such as when he walked through Jericho and saw Zacchaeus. When the woman who has been bleeding touched him, he was on his way to Jairus' house, whose daughter was sick and dying. Jesus walked on water before getting into the boat. He drove the money changers out of the temple. We see the disciples run to the tomb when they hear that Jesus' body is gone. There are so many examples in which heavy work may have had an impact on how the disciples felt and responded in the moment. The proprioceptive (movement) input would have enabled them to feel more regulated, and helped increase their concentration and capacity to learn and take in new information.

The passage at the start of this chapter captures two of the disciples walking along the road to Emmaus with the risen Jesus. They do not initially recognise who he is. It reads that *'beginning with Moses and all the Prophets, he interpreted to them in all the Scriptures the things concerning himself.'* Through the act of walking and talking, the disciples had the opportunity to move and learn and understand more of what God was doing through his son Jesus. In a moment of feeling disheartened, with their *faces downcast* the disciples were able to walk and talk with the risen King and when they arrived at their destination had their eyes open to who they had been sharing their journey with.

The more we do *heavy work* – proprioceptive activities thatput weight through our joints – the more we can help everyone to engage in what is happening. I wonder if this is why Jesus was often on the move as he talked to the disciples. They were often talking and walking, or fishing, or climbing, or in a boat. I don't know if you've noticed, but sometimes it's easier to have a conversation with someone when you're walking along rather than if you're sitting still. I can remember several long walks I've been on where the conversation has become deep and meaningful as we have moved along. I think that is partly due to the regulating ability of proprioceptive input.

We are made to move. We have a God who has given us an amazing body which is designed with joints that can move. We have so much dexterity and ability to do what we do because of the way that our bodies are made and the feedback we receive through our proprioceptive sense when we do them.

Some individuals may have disabilities which prevent them being able to physically move, or from having a good sense of where their body is in space. Some individuals may have a reduced sense of proprioception because of hypermobility (loose ligaments and support around their joints gives them less feedback regarding their body position). These individuals may seek out proprioceptive input by running as hard as they can, throwing themselves to the floor, or doing everything with a great deal of force (like stomping feet, squeezing really hard when opening things, pushing really hard on the page when writing). Whether we can physically move ourselves, seek out lots of movement, or need someone to help us move our limbs, we all have the ability to receive an increased sense of proprioception which can help our awareness of our body position and our self-regulation. For individuals with high levels of physical disability this may look like someone helping them to lie on their tummies and put pressure through the joints in their arms and hands. For individuals who seek out proprioceptive feedback this might look like finding intense movement activities which give them the opportunity to receive this more easily.

We can use movement activities to enable individuals to experience a sense of where their body is in space, to be able to more easily focus on what we're saying or what everyone is learning. I love it when we do this in prayer.-One of the things I've done in kids church with my 6-8 year olds is to pray that God would make us bold and we've taken turns to throw a ball at a giant Jenga tower, then laid hands on each person and prayed for them for boldness.

There are so many examples of churches who have introduced more movement activities into what they are doing and have seen a real increase of individuals being able to participate. Within a church which has a lot of lively boys, they saw an increase in the boys' ability to participate in the Bible teaching and prayer time by changing the way they started the session. They found that if they started the session with everyone pretending to be like a crab, having a slow race across the room, it really helped the rest of the session. By walking on their hands and feet with their bottoms in the air it really helped them all feel more regulated. The ability to receive proprioceptive input through this heavy work activity would have given all the children a greater sense of where their body was in space – a greater sense of being grounded, which would have helped them feel more alert and ready to participate. Once that happened, it was amazing to see the way that all the children engaged with what was going on. They created the story of the Israelites leaving Egypt out of plasticine and then spent time listening to God for the grown-ups in church.

Another church which has several teenagers found that once the youth leaders had an understanding of sensory processing and the impact of movement activities it made a big difference to enabling everyone to participate. The church has one girl, Ali, who has a learning disability and some difficulties in engaging with her peers. She and her mum found that walking the dog and being out and about was a great time to chat to God and mull things over together; to bring their feelings to God, both happy and sad. Ali loves worship. Her group realised that and began to do more activities where everyone could move. This has enabled Ali to start building more friendships with her peers and feel a part of the group.

In a church with a number of adults with mental health needs, they found that the opportunity to participate in small groups such as a cycling group, a running group or a walking group enabled people to more easily share their frustrations, but also engage in conversation about the part God has to play in their lives. Doing physical activities also enabled people to have a sense of satisfaction in participating in something they enjoyed, which helped improve their self esteem.

What about you? I'm sure you have had times in your life where you have felt frustrated, angry, sad, upset or unhappy. For me, when I'm feeling those things, the best thing I can do is to move. I often choose to go for a run when I get up in the morning because I know that will set me up for the day ahead. Not only is it a great way to process how I'm feeling, it also helps me regulate my attention and means I can concentrate on my work for longer. We know that exercise releases endorphins and therefore helps our mood, however it's so much more than that. The movement input and proprioceptive feedback we get from doing something like going on a run, hitting the gym, going for a walk, for a swim, or for a dance, all helps us to self-regulate and gain more of a *just right* level, which then enables us to face the day.

There may be times where you try movement activities and it doesn't quite go to plan. I worked with a lovely little boy, Zach, who has significant autism and cannot speak. When I first met him he was constantly moving around and never stopped. He was unable to sit down at a table even to eat some food. When I started working with him we tried to find movement activities we could put in place which would enable him to feel more regulated and then be able to participate in everyday tasks such as sitting at a table to eat. Within occupational therapy we use several different pieces of equipment (gym balls, scooter boards, lycra tunnels) to help us to do this. The difficulty was that Zach really did not like touch (as we talked about touch sensitivity earlier) and *really* did not like people being near him.

I knew that on a subconscious level Zach was constantly seeking out movement input, so I tried to enable him to access this through equipment in order that he could feel more regulated. To help Zach experience the intensity of *vestibular* and *proprioceptive* input that he could receive by bouncing on a gym ball or rolling on a gym ball, I had to be able to touch him and hold his hips to help him bounce. We started with Zach learning to tolerate being in the same room as the gym ball and then slowly getting near it. There was one session where I tried to show Zach how he could sit on the gym ball. I would usually do this in a way that would mean he could get off really quickly, however, on this occasion I managed to be in a funny position so I could not move out the way quick enough when he had a go. I tried showing Zach how he could sit on the ball and he very decisively bit me on the shoulder to tell me, 'No!' – it was not something he wanted to do!

That was a very painful encounter with trying to enable Zach to have the opportunity for movement activities. Despite that feeling like quite a significant setback, over the next few months we persevered and slowly Zach was able to experience what it felt like to bounce and roll over a gym ball. This helped him with his concentration and he is now able to sit at a table for a meal and for a few minutes of activity with an adult. Zach is now able to use a gym ball to self regulate. He'll choose to go to it himself because he knows it will give him more of an intense experience of movement.

Movement is powerful. Over the next few days perhaps you can reflect on the ways you like to move and how they make you feel. You could also think about how you can increase the opportunity for movement activities both within your services and after them. Tasks such as helping with set-up and pack-down often involve a lot of movement and heavy work and therefore can be an excellent opportunity for regulation.

Chapter 10: Being With
Understanding Our Interoceptive Sense

'As Jesus and his disciples were on their way, he came to a village where a woman named Martha opened her home to him. She had a sister called Mary, who sat at the Lord's feet listening to what he said. But Martha was distracted by all the preparations that had to be made. She came to him and asked, "Lord, don't you care that my sister has left me to do the work by myself? Tell her to help me!" "Martha, Martha," the Lord answered, "you are worried and upset about many things, but few things are needed—or indeed only one. Mary has chosen what is better, and it will not be taken away from her."'
(Luke 10:38-42)

Perhaps, like me, you are someone who picks up people's mannerism and phrases wherever you go. If you spend enough time with someone you tend to start saying the things they say and doing the things they do. When I lived in Northumberland the majority of people spoke with a Geordie accent. After a few months I found myself exclaiming 'Eee' or 'Ah man!' because I heard it so many times from people around me. Now I live in London 'Ah man!' slips out less often. I'm much more likely to say 'Incredible!' – a phrase often repeated in our office at KXC.

When we spend time being with people we often pick up the things they say and do, but we can also pick up their way of living and being. There are times when the feeling of being with certain people has a particular essence to it. Perhaps some people make you feel particularly safe, particularly loved or welcomed. I'm sure there may have been times where a certain place or person has made you feel uneasy. Being able to perceive how we feel when we are with different people or in different environments is part of us being able to process the world around us.

We have an internal eighth sense called *interoception*. This sense is only just starting to be explored and understood by researchers. Interoception is our internal sense of things like whether we need the toilet, whether we are hungry, or whether we feel sick. It tells us if our heart is beating fast or if our tummy feels fluttery – all sensations which are strongly linked to us being able to process and understand our emotions.

As we've already seen, God has given us incredible bodies which have so many capabilities and help us to understand more of him and process the world around us. It is less easy to pin down, but it is also possible that interoception is part of the process of God drawing his people closer to him. Perhaps it was the interoceptive sense that enabled Moses to have a feeling of courage as he stood before the red sea and saw it part. Perhaps it enabled Joshua to have the boldness to speak out *'sun, stand still'* and persevere during the battle with the Amorites. Perhaps it was the interoceptive sense that came over Mary as she *'treasured up all [those] things and pondered them in her heart'* after her encounter with the angel telling her she was to give birth to Jesus. Perhaps it was the interoceptive sense that created a feeling of excitement and anticipation that meant the woman who had been bleeding and Zacchaeus the tax collector sought out Jesus. Perhaps it was the interoceptive sense that overcame Saul as he was struck to the core with what God said to him. From the beginning, God's breath (ruach) his Spirit, was hovering over the waters. The Holy Spirit ministers to and speaks into the heart of God's people throughout the biblical narrative. I wonder if it's partly the interoceptive sense that enables some individuals to sense and act upon these things.

I can recall one specific time where I feel like my interoceptive sense enabled me to know deep peace and the physical feeling of God being with me. During the summer of my second year at university I decided to spend some time volunteering as an occupational therapy student in Thailand. We knew a family who lived there so I went to live with them for seven weeks. On the first day the mum of the family took me to the two locations I was working between – a Thai-run special school and a Christian orphanage for children with additional needs. After that day it was my responsibility, with my broken Thai, to navigate the *songthaew* bus system and get myself to the places where I was working.

At first this went relatively smoothly. I did manage to get lost on my first trip, but a kind *songthaew* driver helped me get to the right place. About a week or two in I was due to meet a friend of a friend for lunch after having done my usual half day in school. I knew that I needed to get on the green *songthaew* (they were colour coded) and ask where it was going. I did this when I got on this bus, however, I found that about 15 minutes into the journey it was not going on its usual route – I looked out of the window and saw that we had suddenly got to a dirt track road, far from the tarmac main road into the city!

In Thailand the *songthaews* are a cross between a bus and a taxi – they go on set routes, but you can hail them and get on and off anywhere you like along the route. When I realised I was in the wrong place I panicked and pressed the button and got off, forgetting that I was actually in (what felt like) the middle of nowhere! It was over thirty degrees and sweltering, but I started to walk back up the road I knew I had come down. I came to a shop where there was one older Thai lady who started talking to me in Thai. My broken Thai was not enough to help me in this situation! She tried to get me to sit down while I tried to explain I was on my way to meet someone. Realising that the friend's friend spoke Thai, I decided to call her and put her on the phone to the Thai shop lady. That worked quite well, except that once I was back on the phone, my friend said to me, 'Where are you? She's speaking northern Thai!' Northern Thai is a dialect not often used in Chiang Mai, which was where I was. I had seemingly managed to cross some kind of language border in going off track. Eventually we realised I could get on a *songthaew* back to the top of the road I had come down and the friend would pick me up from there. After a bit more walking and waiting I made it onto the *songthaew* in the other direction and finally got to meet the friend I had been put in touch with.

The crazy thing is that during this situation, and during some other seemingly out-of-my-depth situations in Thailand, I had a really deep sense of God's peace. I've never had another feeling quite like it before, or since. In the face of circumstances which may have otherwise (and perhaps at times should have) terrified me, I knew that I was meant to be there and that God was with me. Reflecting back on now, I wonder if it was something to do with interoception. It had almost a *physical* feeling of peace, a deep knowing. I wonder if this is the same 'knowing' that Paul talks about when he prays that the Ephesians may *'know the love of Christ that surpasses knowledge'* (Ephesians 3:19).

When I spend time talking to people about hearing God's voice and doing it in a way that is easily accessible, I sometimes talk about having a 'knowing in your knower' – a strong feeling of something. I often feel this at times when I've made big decisions and I just *know* deep down when something is right (often more clearly just after I've made the decision). This has happened to me at key times in my life, such as deciding to move cities, to take jobs, and to launch a charity. When we seek God and ask him to speak to us, he can do so in so many different ways. Sometimes that may be a feeling inside our bodies which gives us a sense of his presence with us and in the things that we are doing.

In order to become like Jesus the disciples spent time being with him. As we spend time being with Jesus he opens our eyes to see things in the way that he sees. I think that it's at these points that we begin to grasp and sense for ourselves his incredible *love surpassing knowledge*. That love which is not just cognitive, but deep within our being. We can start to cultivate this for ourselves and for those around us by choosing to spend time being with Jesus. That will look different for every individual. Perhaps you love being with Jesus in the quiet of a still morning in a comfy chair. Perhaps it's whilst out on a walk or on a run through a forest, or along an ocean path. Perhaps it's whilst singing your heart out to him in a rush hour traffic jam. Perhaps its while you swim, work, paint, dance, ponder or skate. However you choose to spend time with Jesus, let's all choose to do it more. Let's choose to create rhythms where we have the opportunity to be with Jesus, daily. The more we're with Jesus, the more we become like him. The more likely we are to then have that deep sense of knowing of who he is, of seeing the way he sees, and of doing the things that he did.

Mary's reaction to Jesus coming to her sister's home in the passage at the beginning of this chapter shows Mary making a real choice to *be with*. To sit in Jesus' presence and have the opportunity to take in what he was saying. It may have been the interoceptive sense that meant Mary knew she could sit at Jesus' feet and be with him. She possibly had a feeling deep down that enabled her to know that that was okay – that being in Jesus' presence was the best thing to do in that moment. Mary had an opportunity to learn from *being with* Jesus, from sitting in close proximity to him and knowing him with her.

The more we spend time *being with* Jesus, the more we will understand the call he gives us to *be with* people around us. To live in communities in which each and every individual is recognised as being of infinite value to God. This can feel counter cultural in the society we live in. We may need to step out of our own comfort zones to choose to spend time *being with* people who the world may often ignore or put to one side.

It is through choosing to *be with* and spend time with individuals with significant levels of disability that I feel I have more deeply learnt what it is to *be with* Jesus and spend time in his presence. I had the honour of meeting and hanging out with two incredible girls, Anna and Lydia, both of whom had really significant physical disabilities. They needed support from adults to do all the things that we do every day – washing, dressing, eating, playing, moving. I met Anna and Lydia when I was a teenager helping to support children within the Our Place venue (for children with additional needs) at United. I absolutely loved being allocated to be with them. We would sit and read stories and just spend time with them lying on the floor out of their wheelchairs. What was most encouraging and inspiring was that both Anna and Lydia had a deep sense of God's peace and presence that they carried with them. Spending time being with them taught me what it is to carry a peace in the essence of your being. Anna and Lydia embodied God's presence more than anyone else I've met.

You may have read *Adam, God's beloved* by Henri Nouwen. He describes a similar process of learning through the opportunity of being with Adam, a young adult with significant disabilities. Although the world may struggle to look beyond physical disability, God offers the opportunity for everyone to live in relationship with him. Individuals who embody God's presence so strongly challenge us in the way we spend time being with Jesus and living life as his disciples. I long to be someone who embodies that sense of God's presence because of the time I have spent being with Jesus. Over the next week maybe you could carve out a bit of time each day to practise being with God. Choose to spend time in Jesus' presence and then respond to what he speaks to you during that time. Ask him to open your eyes to see the people he is calling you to be with in the community around you.

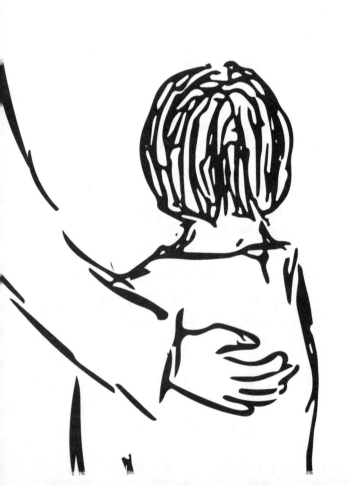

Chapter 11: From the Youngest
Supporting Children and Young People

Jesus welcomes children
'Then people brought little children to Jesus for him to place his hands on them and pray for them. But the disciples rebuked them. Jesus said, "Let the little children come to me, and do not hinder them, for the kingdom of heaven belongs to such as these." When he had placed his hands on them, he went on from there.'
(Matthew 19:13-15)

The kingdom of heaven belongs to those who are like children. What does Jesus mean when he proclaims this? Jesus is painting a picture of what it is like to enter into his presence. When we come to God with the purity, energy and longing of a child, he loves it. The passage above in Matthew 19 is another reminder of Jesus being counter cultural. As we can see from verse 13, those bringing the children to Jesus were rebuked by the disciples. Within their culture, children were viewed as less important. Jesus is yet again turning this view on its head and demonstrating the radical welcome that he brings.

We should welcome children just as Jesus welcomes them. To welcome everyone into our church communities, including the very youngest, is so important. Whether you are a church member, a teenager, a church leader or a volunteer, the welcome we give can have a big impact on every individual we come across. One of the things I absolutely love doing at church on a Sunday is greeting both the parents and children. I love getting down to a child's level and asking them about their week, the toy they're holding, the holiday they've been on, or what they've been playing with their friends. Taking the time to say hello and have a conversation with the children I meet speaks value over them. It shows them (and their parents) that I care about how they are doing; about what they think. I believe this is a reflection of how God sees them. He cares about all children; about how they are, what they think, how they are connecting with him and the people around them.

Choosing to do this may feel a bit strange at first. It may feel like trying to have an adult conversation with a child. Children are different from adults and there are lots of things that you would not ask or chat about in the same way. However, their opinion is just as valid. Children are able to tell you about their week, to say hello, to tell you something about what they're thinking if you take time to ask them.

If there isn't a culture of welcome and talking to children in your church this is a great place to start! It is something that can quite easily be changed within church culture. If everyone takes time to have a conversation with at least one child when they're welcoming on a Sunday it will start to change the way children are seen and valued. It's very easy to slip into an attitude of adult conversations being the most important. I remember countless Sundays as a child where I would be hanging off my mum or tugging her sleeve because I wanted to be talked to as well, or I'd decided it was time to go home because no one was talking to me! Both conversations are important – those with adults and those with children. Let's try to create a culture where both can happen and everyone is valued for what they bring to the community they are in.

One thing we know about all of the senses we've talked about is that they are foundational to the way we experience the world. Some occupational therapy researchers have drawn this diagrammatically with a triangle. They show us that the senses we have are the base of everything we do. The first three senses to develop are our *tactile* (touch), *vestibular* (balance) and *proprioceptive* (body awareness) senses. These are at the base of the triangle. Then our sight, hearing, smell and taste senses are on the rung above. Above these are all the things that we do with our bodies, such as using two hands together, having hand-eye coordination, managing our behaviour. Then academic learning right at the top. First and foremost we experience and process the world through our senses. If we are not enabling individuals to engage with their senses or get to a level where they feel 'just right' and can process the world around them, they are less likely to be able to take in and process what we are doing.

I love the insight that knowing about sensory processing give us. It enables us to more easily understand why people behave in the way they do. Sensory processing is not everything, there are lots of other things which will have an impact on the way we behave and the reason we do the things that we do. However, if we have this triangle in mind we know that we use our senses all the time to make sense of the world around us.

These senses are important not just to individuals with additional needs, and not just to children, but to all of us.

This is a challenge to the way we think about and plan the teaching we do, and the way that we facilitate and recognise others engaging with God and going deeper in their walk with Jesus. When we are with children, they are still learning and developing their ability to understand and process all the different sensory experiences the world throws at them. From the moment we are born we start to process things through our senses. We learn how to feel and understand the shape of objects through putting them in our mouths. We learn how to process different textures by crawling on the floor. We have a reflex that means as a baby our head turns to look at our outstretched hand. This helps us to learn that we can use our hands and eyes together and that our hands can have an effect on objects that we touch. Children love to explore – they are constantly learning and taking in the world around them. Thinking about the different ways in which we process the world through our senses (sight, sound, smell, taste, touch, movement, body awareness, interoception) can help children explore their relationship with God. Just as Jesus says, *'the kingdom of heaven belongs to such as these'*, I wonder if he is in part referring to children's ability to explore and be open to the world around them.

The best way to support children with additional needs in our churches is to make changes for all the children that involve ways of exploring the world through the bodies God has given us. We have talked through lots of practical suggestions as we've gone through this book, but I'm going to try and summarise some of the ideas and how they specifically apply to children with additional needs. There may be some strategies that you use for certain children, however, as a general rule it is helpful to have all resources available to everyone. If your teaching can enable all children to participate then that is incredible, and I think a great reflection of Jesus' heart for all.

Just a little aside: people often ask me what happens when one child needs a certain piece of equipment. 'Don't all the other children ask for a go?' Sometimes they might, but more often than not children are much more tolerant of different things than we realise. It can be helpful to explain things to them like this: 'Just like I need glasses to help me see, Jonny needs this cushion to help him to listen to the story.' Children tend to accept a statement like that. There may be times where they are adamant they would like a go, and in that case I would let them have a turn and then make sure the piece of equipment goes back to the child who needs it. All the strategies I've referred to are not going to do any harm to a child who does not specifically need them, therefore if you have more than one of everything you can share the spares around each week.

As adults I think that sometimes it is us who struggle with some children doing things differently. If we think about our own reaction, we can think about what is reasonable and what may be unreasonable to expect of children. For example, lots of children benefit from the use of what we call a *fidget*. A fidget is a small toy, such as a tangle or twist 'n' lock blocks – something you can hold in your hands. Fidgets helps to keep the proprioceptive and tactile senses active when we're trying to listen. It can enable children to get to a *just right* level for learning. I wonder if you ever doodle or chew gum to help you concentrate? If you do, it's probably a subconscious strategy, but it is a strategy you are using to help yourself stay alert. If we give children equipment such as fidgets to help them to stay alert this can enable them to engage for longer. This might mean that a child looks at the fidget and not us, but quite often this enables them to listen for longer. You can set simple rules for using fidgets such as, 'This fidget is to help you to concentrate so that moving your hands helps your brain stay switched on, but if you choose to throw it I will take it away.' Often, for us as adults, it's being able to turn off the idea that everyone must be totally still and looking at us if they are listening. There will be times when using a whispered but excited voice to try and help everyone look with their eyes and listen with their ears is helpful. But it is good to bear in mind that children can listen when they're not looking at us too.

Here are some specific ideas and pointers for children with additional needs:

See differently

- Think about where children are sitting. If you have children in your group who love *visual* detail (this is often the case for children with autism) they may benefit from being near the front so there is less visual distraction between them and you as a leader.

- Think about how Jesus' used people's sight to help them to engage in a story, such as *'look at the birds'*. How can you engage children in looking at things which may help them understand more of what God might want to say to them? For children who cannot physically see or who have limited vision, you can put adaptations in place to help them. This might include a different feeling cushion which they always sit on, braille resources, or objects that they can feel to engage in the story. Also useful is high contrast and large print song words for worship and any paper based activity.

Recognise God's voice

- God wants us all to be able to hear his voice. We can talk to children about the different ways that we can 'hear' God speaking to us. This might be audibly, but more often than not it can be through one of our other senses or through a thought in our brain.

- Talk to children to help them have more opportunity to hear, understand and grow in their faith. We can think about the way that we use our voice to engage individuals. A steady calm voice can be calming, a quick paced, higher tone voice can be alerting. If we whisper then children will lean in to hear; if we shout children will just talk louder.

- If children are very young or have a learning disability then simple language can really help them to understand. Think about the words you use – nothing too long! Regularly check in with children to ask them if they know what certain words mean (sin, forgive, compassion, grace and love are all words we might automatically use but children often might not understand). Using a child's name before a command will help them to know you're talking to them: *'Naomi, sitting'* and a visual indication of what I'd like Naomi to do is much easier than *'It's time for us to sit down. Can you come and sit down next to me in the circle Naomi?'*

- Speech and language therapists often talk about something called a *total communication approach*. This means giving as many clues as possible as to what you're saying in order that everyone can understand. This might mean using pictures, using objects to represent things you are talking about, and using Makaton sign language alongside your speech and worship to help everyone understand.

- For children who cannot hear or have limited hearing it's really important to think about how they will engage in the session. If you can get someone to interpret BSL then do. Think about how you communicate through other senses, have written words, pictures, videos to demonstrate what you're talking about to help with understanding.

Smell and remember

- We've thought about how important our sense of smell can be to help us create memories. Think about the smell of each story that you're teaching. Is there a way you can bring smell into how you are engaging the children around you?

- If children are hypersensitive to smell this can impact their ability to participate. Be aware that this could be a problem for some children – you can be creative in how you overcome it!

Taste and see the Lord is good

- Our mouth is a powerful sensory regulator. Bringing in crunchy snacks (when children are old enough to manage them) such as breadsticks, carrot pieces, apple pieces etc can be a great way to enable everyone to feel more regulated and therefore engage.

- We can *taste and see the Lord is good* (Psalm 34:8). Are there ways that you could bring taste into what you're doing on a Sunday?

Transforming touch

- Touch is one of our most important senses. Could you use touch to help children to understand more of what God is saying? What does the story feel like? Was there dirt on the floor? Was there bark on the tree? What did the material of the clothes feel like? Were there woolly sheep?

- Using different objects, smells, tastes etc., in our story can provide lots of different props to help children understand. A story box in which you put everything for your story can help everyone be more engaged. Starting a story with a whispered, *'Who would like to come and see what's in my box?'* motivates and interests children. Use this as an opportunity to ask children you know need to move or stay engaged to come and look, and choose something out of your box.

- *Deep pressure* touch is easier to understand. When we're guiding children with touch, a firm hand on the shoulder is much easier to process than a brush past them.

- Some children and young people will find touch very difficult to process. If a child is adopted or fostered or has a known sensitivity to touch, talk to their parent or carer about what is most helpful for them.

Gaining balance

- Just as Jesus reminded the disciples of the stillness and peace he brings during a storm, we can use movement and pauses within what we're doing to help everyone understand.

- There are times when it can help to be still. We can take time to be still as we listen to God in what we are doing and teaching. We can try and incorporate moments where all the children take a pause to regain their balance and listen to Jesus. (You can do this by all lying on the floor, putting on a piece of music or waving a parachute over everyone whilst listening to what God is saying. I've done this with 1-3yr olds and it's amazing to see them engage in what God is saying).

- We know linear movement is calming. If you have children who love to spin or hang upside down they might really benefit from linear movement activities within the session (e.g. jumping on a trampoline, bouncing on a gym ball, or if they're small, swinging in a blanket).

Made to move

- *Proprioception* (body awareness) is gained through *heavy work*. This is a really important sense to understand because we know that it is regulating for our bodies.

- The more proprioceptive activities we incorporate into what we do with children and young people the more regulated they will be and the easier it will be for them to participate. (Try interchanging movement activity with focused activity – things like worship and teaching and prayer can all involve movement. Specific *movement breaks* might be walking like an animal, pushing the wall, jumping up and down, giving yourself a big hug).

- Some children will seek out movement more than others. Whether children have a diagnosed need (such as Autism,

ADHD or Foetal Alcohol Syndrome) or no diagnosed need, children who are constantly on the go love falling to the floor, cannot sit still, are seeking out movement. The more movement we put into everything we're doing the more we will help these individuals feel regulated and able to participate.

- Some children will avoid movement and may appear floppy or bored a lot of the time. Enabling these children to move with an engaging activity (such as dancing to a song like *Let's get ready to rumble*) and moving in the same ways as suggested above can also help these children to engage.

- Some children may have a physical disability which makes movement difficult for them. This can mean that children struggle with standing up for singing time, moving their body for actions or using their hands for craft. Enabling children to physically have a go at activities is important. Ask parents and carers how you can facilitate movement for individual children. As a general guide, you can support children physically at big joints (e.g. you would support a child who needs extra stability for sitting or standing at their hips). If a child is sitting down and cannot physically do an activity you can use a *hand over hand* approach. Use your hands over the child's hands to help them do something (for example using a glue stick or scissors).

Being with

- As we spend time ourselves *being with* Jesus, we will be able to grasp more of his heart and the way that he wants us to respond to people around us.

- *Being with* children and young people who have additional needs can be challenging but also so rewarding. When we're with children who seem to be doing things differently to everyone else, we can be asking God to show us what it is that he loves and values about the child we're with. Often, in taking time to be with children, we come to understand something more of them and something more of God and how he is speaking to them.

- As we take time to be with the children and young people we are coming alongside, it is really important that we think about how engaging we are. Having a clear plan (lay this out with a *visual schedule* of laminated symbols) helps everyone to know what they are doing and when. Just as you or I might love to have our diaries and know what we're doing, this can help every child and young person (and us as leaders) follow a session. Keeping everything engaging is also really important. If we can smoothly move from one activity to another (which we can do by using the language *'Story is finished, now it's singing time'*) we don't lose any children while we are looking for our notes or deciding what to do next.

These are all strategies we often put in place with the children and young people with additional needs that we support through Our Place at United in the summer. If you ever want to learn more or practise putting these strategies in place you can come and see what we do or come on a team and have a go!

It is through being on a team that several individuals have had the opportunity to practise strategies that they have then been able to take home and use in their churches.

When churches take on board accessibility for children in their kids ministry, it can make a big difference to how everyone participates. One church has quite a few children with additional needs attending. The kids pastor takes assemblies at the church school nearby and often had questions from a little boy called Ben who doesn't have a church background. Ben was so curious about God that he talked to his mum, Sophie, about going to church. Ben and Sophie popped in during the week and met one of the church staff members who chatted with them about what Ben's interests were and what would help him to be able to feel safe on a Sunday. They agreed together that Ben would either like to sit in the congregation, by the band (because he loves music), or by the sound desk (because he loves seeing how this works). Ben has autism and anxiety, which makes it difficult to go to new and busy places. The staff member made sure that both the vicar and the kids pastor knew that the family might be coming on Sunday, so that church could be a welcoming place for Ben and Sophie.

Sunday came and the vicar was able to spot Ben and Sophie when they arrived and greet them by name. The kids pastor also met them and helped to explain what would happen during the service and ask Ben what he would like to do. Ben chose to go to the sound desk. He was introduced to the lady who was running it and she adopted him as her apprentice for the day. Sophie and Ben were overwhelmed with the welcome they received, coming for the first time. Ben kept exclaiming, *'This church is amazing!'*

At another church a child with significant autism who was non-verbal came on a Sunday without any prior warning. Instead of panicking, the leader continued as normal, being welcoming, praying and doing their best to include. This meant that the family knew they were welcome. The leaders were then able to seek help and training to support the child even more on a Sunday.

As part of Growing Hope King's Cross I work on a Sunday to enable children that we provide therapy for within clinic, and their families, to have the opportunity to access and participate in church. One child, Noah, had been part of church all his life, but found it really tricky to sit down for story and to engage in the same activities as the other children. With a bit more support – a visual schedule so he knew what was happening when; a wobble cushion he could sit on; and a fidget he could hold so he could move a bit during story – he was able to join in with everything that was happening. Noah's parents were amazed at the transformation in his ability to sit and listen and join in with everyone else. Noah absolutely loves coming along and playing with everyone and it's been great to see him thriving as a part of kids ministry.

At another church there is a family who have been coming along as a result of parenting courses and toddler church. They have a little boy called Josh who was diagnosed with autism at around 18 months. For a while, Josh and his family did not go to anything at church because his behaviour was challenging. As Josh got older he came to toddler church because it was a relaxed and open space where he did not have to conform to anything, but he could be there and engage as he wanted to.

The summer after Josh started school he went along to the church's holiday club and had the best time! The church had made sure that an experienced one-on-one volunteer was there to support him. They had prepared some teaching that would help him to learn and engage. Josh absolutely loved it and continued to talk about the holiday club over six months later.

The following September, Josh was old enough to start coming to the kids group on a Sunday. Josh's parents were worried about him coming and that his behaviour would be too challenging. They offered to accompany him, but the church was able to provide one-to-one support which has worked really well. As well as an adult one-to-one, the church has supported and trained a teenager to be with Josh, which has become a lovely relationship. Josh does not remember most people's names, but he will ask for both of his one-to-ones by name and will talk about them during the week. Josh's family say that he looks forward to participating in kid's club all week. Josh is able to join in with the games and quieter bits and then at other times he'll play with his one-to-one or run and climb in the room. Although it appears that Josh is not taking much in, he always is. Often Josh will say things which surprise the leaders, because he's heard more than he appears to and will refer back to it. Josh's mum has sent a picture of him retelling one of the Bible stories he'd heard in church to his toys at home. It has been amazing how the church has journeyed with Josh and his family and have enabled him to truly participate, enjoy and grow in his relationship with God!

It is also through practical training which looks at the things we have talked through in this book that enables small changes to make a big difference to children's understanding. By using multisensory strategies and creative ways of engaging individuals everyone is more able to participate alongside each other. I have been told the story of one church who, following training, made changes towards doing more multisensory and accessible worship, teaching and prayer ministry times. They found that all the children were more engaged and enjoyed coming along on a Sunday and that children were able to articulate more what God was saying to them.

So it's time to start. If your kids ministry does not already use some of the strategies talked about above, let's choose to start putting them in place. Perhaps look at your programme (or look at appendices 4 and 5 for some more examples and ideas) and try and change one or two things to make them more accessible for all children. What is great about kids and young people's ministry is that the more multisensory we are, the better. It's much easier to adapt and remain age appropriate compared to adult ministry. We do need to target the activities to the age and the personalities of the children and young people we're alongside, but often the more active we are the better!

Chapter 12: To The Oldest
Supporting Youth and Adults

'Now there was a man in Jerusalem called Simeon, who was
righteous and devout. He was waiting for the consolation of
Israel, and the Holy Spirit was on him. It had been revealed to
him by the Holy Spirit that he would not die before he had seen
the Lord's Messiah. Moved by the Spirit, he went into the temple
courts. When the parents brought in the child Jesus to do for
him what the custom of the Law required, Simeon took him in
his arms and praised God, saying: "Sovereign Lord, as you have
promised, you may now dismiss your servant in peace. For my
eyes have seen your salvation, which you have prepared in the
sight of all nations: a light for revelation to the Gentiles, and the
glory of your people Israel."*

*The child's father and mother marvelled at what was said about
him. Then Simeon blessed them and said to Mary, his mother:
"This child is destined to cause the falling and rising of many
in Israel, and to be a sign that will be spoken against, so that
the thoughts of many hearts will be revealed. And a sword will
pierce your own soul too."*

*There was also a prophet, Anna, the daughter of Penuel, of the
tribe of Asher. She was very old; she had lived with her husband*

Love Surpassing Knowledge

seven years after her marriage, and then was a widow until she
was eighty-four. She never left the temple but worshiped night
and day, fasting and praying. Coming up to them at that very
moment, she gave thanks to God and spoke about the child to
all who were looking forward to the redemption of Jerusalem.

(Luke 2:25-38)

God is a God who draws us all into relationship with him, from
the youngest to the oldest. I love the story of Simeon and Anna
who knew the Holy Spirit's voice and heard God speaking to
them about the birth of Jesus. At the birth of a tiny baby God
spoke to so many different people who may have not been an
expected part of his kingdom. God announced the birth to the
shepherds (who were often ostracised and looked down upon
in ancient middle eastern community), spoke to the Magi
(who did not have a Jewish background, as would have been
expected of those to whom God spoke about the Messiah), and
appointed Simeon and Anna, both older in age. The range of
people that God used to witness and celebrate the birth of his
son Jesus, our Messiah and King, demonstrates his heart for all
people across ages, cultures, abilities and stages of life. I love
that, time and again, God does this throughout the Bible.

This chapter aims to summarise and explore practically how
we can enable young people and adults with additional needs
to participate in our church communities. Often it can feel
easier to include children, because many of the multisensory
strategies are more adaptable for children, but less acceptable
for older youth or adults. The question of how to apply all this
to adults is often asked and hopefully will be answered to some
extent here.

Here are some specific ideas and pointers for young people and adults with additional needs:

See differently

- Think about where individuals are sitting. Those who find visual information distracting may like to sit nearer the front so they can engage more easily.

- Use visual illustrations – images and short video clips that support what you are saying can go a long way.

- Images can be a really helpful way of enabling everyone to participate in a discussion. If you are running a small group with young people or adults with learning disabilities, using images enables concepts to be more easily understood and discussed. For example, if you are talking about God's love you could use pictures of a gift, a hug, arms wide open, or a family, as a basis for discussion. An individual with a learning disability could choose a picture as a way of participating in a discussion, even if they cannot verbally articulate this. Other members of the group could both choose a picture and verbally explain and discuss their choice.

- For adults who cannot physically see or who have limited vision, you can put adaptations in place to help them. This might include: a certain chair that is reserved for them, so they know where they're going when they arrive; someone on the welcome team who has been trained to guide; braille resources or objects that individuals can feel to engage in the talk or discussion; high contrast and large print song words for worship and any paper-based activity. Thinking about the small things (such as a bowl of water for guide dogs) can help individuals know they are welcome.

Recognise God's voice

- God wants us all to be able to hear his voice. We can practically teach youth and adults about ways that we can 'hear' God speaking. This may be audibly, but it could be through another of our senses. Regularly reminding people of this can enable everyone to feel they have the opportunity to participate.

- Use your voice to be engaging. We all can engage more if someone is animated. Using your facial expressions, body language, visual and physical props puts in place a *total communication approach,* which more individuals will be motivated to listen to and then be more able to understand. Change of pace, volume and pitch of voice can help draw people in.

- Adapt your language. Think about the individuals who could be coming into your church. If we are to be a church that is accessible to everyone, we may have youth or adults with learning disabilities, or who simply do not have a church background and therefore don't understand the language we use. Even if a concept appears simple to you (e.g. grace, sin, compassion, forgiveness, reconciliation) always explain what it is that you mean.

- For youth or adults who cannot hear or have limited hearing, think about adaptations that can be put in place. Do you have a hearing loop? Can you find BSL interpreters to interpret for individuals who use BSL? Could you provide more written information that enables individuals to follow what is happening?

Smell and remember

- We've thought about how important our sense of smell can be to help us create memories. How could you use smell in what you are doing with adults to help them to remember (e.g. to give them something like chocolate to smell, taste and remember God's goodness; you could use a scented candle to draw them into the smell of a particular Bible passage such as when Zaccheaus climbs the sycamore tree).

- Some individuals may be sensitive to smell and this can impact their ability to participate, so always give opportunities for youth and adults to talk about what might help them to engage more. If you have a nominated individual who oversees accessibility they can become a point of contact for adults being able to say what they need.

Taste and see the Lord is good

- When we are bored we often touch our mouths or lean our chin on our hands subconsciously, because our mouth is a sensory regulator. You could incorporate crunchy or chewy snacks into what you do so that everyone can be more regulated and ready to listen and learn (for example, carrot sticks and apples alongside pastries or doughnuts at coffee; chewy sweets that are passed around in a break).

- Like smell, taste can help us to connect with the story. Perhaps if you run a small group in which you eat as part of your evening you could think about tastes that are involved in the passage you are discussing and link this in.

Transforming touch

- Touch is one of our most important senses. If we are creative there are ways in which we can enable youth and adults to be drawn deeper into what God is saying through communicating what it might have *felt like* to be a part of the Bible passage we're teaching. Giving everyone something to hold, such as a bit of twig, a piece of fake grass, a piece of cloth, that could enable a deeper connection with what God is saying through a passage. If this isn't possible for everyone, you could think about which aspects of what is being said could be tactile. As people are welcomed into church, give them the opportunity to pick up something to hold from a basket by the door if they would like to.

- Doodling and fidgeting can help us to self-regulate and therefore concentrate more easily on what is going on. Creating an atmosphere where it's okay to have a pen and paper or something in your hands can be helpful. Having objects such as pipe cleaners or tangles or a small piece of clay or a stone on people's chairs can give them something to keep their hands busy and therefore focus more easily.

- Deep pressure touch is easier to understand. When we're using touch to help youth or adults with additional needs to move to a new space, a firm hand on the shoulder is much easier to process than a brush past them.

- Some youth and adults find touch very difficult to process. Have a conversation with them or their carer about what they like or do not like. If an individual tells you that they do not like touch, be aware of this. Sometimes, the more tactile among us, without thinking, might put a hand on a shoulder or an arm and for some individuals this can feel uncomfortable.

Gaining balance

- Movement activities become quite difficult with youth and adults as they often appear less likely to want to move than children.

- Encouraging moments where everyone collectively takes time to *be still* can be a powerful way of individuals being able to slow down and recalibrate their vestibular system. This could be done through a short time of silence or a quiet song in which everyone has the opportunity to *be still*.

- For individuals with significant additional needs who are often spinning round or trying to hang upside down, linear movement is calming. Enabling individuals to have access to a mini trampoline for jumping on could be helpful. Perhaps less intrusive might be enabling individuals to sit on a gym ball if they would like to. Gym balls are great because they're easy to sit on, bounce on and roll over (all of which can be calming for our vestibular systems). Gym balls can also be a more comfy seat for anyone as they prompt an upright posture.

- As we get older our sense of balance often diminishes. Practically we can make sure that we have pathways clear of slippy rugs or trailing wires, and well-marked changes in levels of the floor (yellow tape can work well) to help make sure that everyone has the opportunity to keep their balance. Having two banisters rather than one on the stairs can help individuals with physical needs get up and down more easily. Having a rail next to the toilet so that individuals can get up and down more easily can be helpful. Making sure there is space for individuals to use crutches, sticks or walkers is also really important.

Made to move

- Proprioception (body awareness) is gained through *heavy work*. This is a really important sense to understand because we know that it is regulating for our bodies.

- The more proprioceptive activities we incorporate into what we do with youth and adults the better. This not only enables youth and adults with additional needs to feel more regulated, but helps every individual to be able to focus and participate more easily.

- We have to be creative about the ways in which we create movement activities, so that they are more age appropriate. Activities could include moving chairs into a circle for discussion, asking specific individuals to come and help hold something, or to carry water jugs to fill the urn (because carrying something heavy puts pressure through our joints and therefore gives us proprioceptive feedback). We could use active songs that we do as a whole church (such as action songs or songs that everyone signs to). We could use a game or a passage in which we challenge everyone to stand up and sit back down every time they hear a certain word.

- Enable opportunities for breaks to move within services or groups. You could have a break to grab a cup of tea or go to the toilet if you need to. You could ask individuals you know need movement to pass the collection basket round or do a practical role that enables them to move. When you have ministry time you could give everyone the opportunity to respond through moving.

- For youth and adults who find it difficult to move we can think about ways in which we make sure they are still able to participate. Is there space for individuals to move forward for prayer if they are using a walker or a wheelchair? Is there a way of individuals with physical disabilities to go onto the stage, or be shown on the screen if they are talking from the front? Are other practical things in place for physical access (ramps to get in, accessible toilets etc.)?

Being with

- The more we spend time *being with* Jesus the more we are able to grasp his heart for the people around us. no matter what their additional needs.

- Being with youth and adults with additional needs can be both challenging and rewarding. Through spending time being with individuals who may initially seem different to us we can start to see, recognise and celebrate what God has put in each and every individual.

- Sometimes 'being with' may look like being an individual who comes alongside an adult with additional needs, sitting with them and explaining what is happening in a session or service. For some adults with mental health needs or learning disabilities, a talk can be too fast-paced and difficult to understand. Sitting with an individual and drawing out what is being talked about on a whiteboard or paper, and writing simple sentences that help explain what is being discussed, can help some adults to participate. (This can be facilitated within the church community by having white boards and pens that individuals can use or by equipping the welcome team to know how to come alongside and support adults if they need it).

- Taking time to be with the youth and adults with additional needs in our church communities means using as many strategies as possible to help everyone participate. Something which can really help all of us and may be particularly helpful for individuals with anxiety or a need for structure and routine is a service sheet. This becomes a visual schedule that helps individuals to track through what is happening during that meeting or session. It might be that, rather than giving this to everyone, you have a few copies of the plan by the door so that people who need this have the opportunity to access it. An easy-read version that everyone can access might be helpful (see example in Appendix 7) giving an outline of what is happening which also uses symbols in order that everyone can see and understand it.

These are all strategies we put in place within Access, the team who support adults with additional needs to be able to participate in everything going on at United. It is amazing to see the difference this makes to individuals being able to participate. As a team we have seen a lady called Lucy, who has complex mental health needs, be supported to volunteer on a team and access the main worship celebrations. Lucy mainly needs someone to come alongside her and explain what is happening and to make sure she has everything she needs to be able to understand. When she's in a main session Lucy likes to sit near to the Access team, so she knows she has support if she needs it, but is otherwise happy knowing people are near by. Other adults, such as Matt, need a bit more support to engage. The team enabled Matt to have the opportunity to move during worship and to feel safe within a space towards the back of the congregation. During the talk, the team used simple words, drawings and objects to help Matt have an opportunity to connect with God. Matt has a significant learning disability and therefore most of his learning is at a sensory level: he is able to connect with God and engage through exploring objects and participating in movement activities. The team therefore applied what was being said to a simple sentence or phrase which could sum up the truth being preached. Another individual, John, absolutely loved being in the heart of worship and a member of the team would go to the front with him so that he could dance and join in. They would then support him to understand what was being talked about through drawing it out and explaining it in a discussion after the talk.

It is great to see churches apply this to their ministry on a Sunday and during the week. One church has a fifteen year old with Aspergers called Charlie, who goes along to their youth ministry. When the youth team found out that Charlie was coming along they were worried about how they would handle things and help him to participate. The team were generally very nervous and this made it difficult to feel that it would be okay. Thankfully, one member of the team already knew

Charlie well, which was helpful in enabling him to participate. The leader of the youth team made sure that they connected well with Charlie's mum beforehand, so that she could talk to them if she had any concerns, or if Charlie let her know he had concerns. When Charlie started coming along the team gave him a single leader who was his point of contact, so that if he was uncomfortable about anything he had someone he could talk to. Charlie and his mum agreed with the leaders that he could leave at any time if he would like to.

As Charlie started coming, the leaders did not ask too much of him. As he became more comfortable, he appeared to enjoy participating in the group, being sparky and sarcastic, asking challenging questions which made his intelligence clear. The other youth had some challenges with understanding Charlie's social skills, but the youth leaders took time to talk to the young people about autism so that they could understand and about kindness and how we can respond when we find things difficult. There are times when Charlie will need advance warning of an activity, or an explanation of what is about to happen, but otherwise he participates alongside everyone else. It is difficult to know what Charlie is thinking or feeling, but the youth leaders check in with him every so often and more often than not he is doing well. Charlie's mum has let the youth leaders know that going along to youth is one part of the week that he does not want to miss. Charlie will prepare to go well before he needs to, because he loves the chance to go. The youth leaders found that they didn't need to do anything particularly different to enable Charlie to be a part of their group and it's amazing to see the way in which he is growing in his relationship with God through the opportunity to be there.

Practically, putting these strategies in place and helping youth and adults to participate can make it a challenge to have appropriate boundaries in place. As we talked about in chapter three, if we create a community around vulnerable youth and adults with additional needs, we can help support everyone in a way that is safe. Often, if you are an individual who has enabled participation to be easier, it can lead to youth or adults wanting to always talk to you or to have your help when they are stuck. Through making sure that you work as a team and that all of the welcome team and church community can take responsibility for everyone being able to access church, we can avoid one person feeling responsible and becoming overwhelmed by an individual's needs.

Let's choose to give this a go. Lots of the strategies that we have talked about are easily implemented on a Sunday or within your church community and therefore enable more people to access what is going on. Perhaps look at your teaching or service plans (or look at Appendix 6 for some more examples and ideas) and try and change one or two things to make them more accessible for all youth and adults. Don't forget how important movement is. The more we incorporate opportunities for movement, the more individuals will be able to participate.

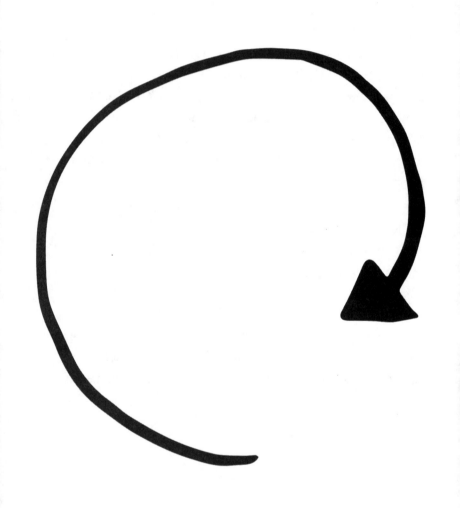

Chapter 13: More

'For this reason I kneel before the Father, from whom every family in heaven and on earth derives its name. I pray that out of his glorious riches he may strengthen you with power through his Spirit in your inner being, so that Christ may dwell in your hearts through faith. And I pray that you, being rooted and established in love, may have power, together with all the Lord's holy people, to grasp how wide and long and high and deep is the love of Christ, and to know this love that surpasses knowledge—that you may be filled to the measure of all the fullness of God.

Now to him who is able to do immeasurably more than all we ask or imagine, according to his power that is at work within us, to him be glory in the church and in Christ Jesus throughout all generations, for ever and ever! Amen.'

(Ephesians 3:14-20)

Wherever we start, God promises that he will do immeasurably more than we could ask or imagine. Perhaps pause now and spend 10 minutes with a piece of paper dreaming what it could look like if everyone with additional needs was welcome in the way that God welcomes. I wonder what that picture looks like?

Immeasurably more – it's a tricky concept to get our heads around. We probably don't know what immeasurably more looks like because our brains only take us so far. Look at the picture that you've painted or dreamt. God can do immeasurably more than we ask or imagine.

I would love it if we start to see more of what Paul captures in this Ephesians 3 passage. That we would see church communities full of people who are filled with the power of God's Spirit in their inner being. That we would become a people who are rooted in Christ's love. That we would have a deep knowledge of that love, not just a cognitive knowledge, but based on relationship which surpasses knowledge. That we would be a community that endlessly welcomes and grows because it is full of individuals who are walking steadfastly in that deep knowledge of God's love. A community of people who look outwards at others rather than inwards at themselves. A community of people who recognise and accept the unique gifts, skills and calling that God has put within each and every individual. A community that does not leave individuals on the edge. A community where every single person feels like they are part of the family. If we become a church that looks like this, it could have the potential to shift the culture of our local communities and our nation.

As a young teenager, when I first had an interest in additional needs ministry and started to support a few individuals, I had no idea where that would lead me. I love that I have been able to study occupational therapy and gain an understanding which is so applicable to enabling everyone to participate in church. It has been amazing to see the accessible church ministry grow within New Wine churches – not just at the summer gatherings, but in churches across the country. It has been great to see accessibility talked about more as it has moved closer to the top of church agendas over the last ten years. Culture so often looks upon disability as 'us' (without a disability) and 'them' (with a disability), but as a church it feels as though we are on the edge of a shift in culture that is moving away from a sense of *us* and *them* towards a sense of *together*.

There are countless churches where we have seen individuals learn how to support and welcome one family or one vulnerable adult with additional needs. This learning has then enabled these churches to open their doors to more individuals with additional needs. When one family is welcomed, they tend to invite along other families who may previously have felt like they didn't have the opportunity to be part of a church.

One story that captures this is of a church where inclusion support at their local holiday club led to a family feeling like they could come along to church on a Sunday. As this family started to attend, the kids team were able to become more equipped. They built and trained a team so that more individuals with additional needs could come along. The church then found that more families started to come along who had children with additional needs.

One family have a little boy called Keshav who has autism. Keshav has limited language, but each time he comes to church he repeats words like 'church', 'God' and 'Jesus' when he is interacting with people around him. On remembrance Sunday Keshav was in church with his family during the two minute silence and was continuing to say 'church', 'God' and 'Jesus'. The amazing thing was that the whole church family were so tuned into being able to welcome and accept *everyone* as part of the church community, that no one minded Keshav talking and no one complained about him making a noise during the silence.

So many times I have heard of churches who have decided to step into trying to make things more accessible. They have sought out training, given things a go, and have seen families and individuals who may not otherwise have been able to be part of church to be included. It does not always look the way we think it will look, but God can always do immeasurably more when we take the time to set fires and step out and see what happens.

As we start to capture what it looks like in God's kingdom, as we see a true picture of the infinite value and love that he speaks over every individual in our world, we can see things start to shift in our communities and cultures. Whether you are starting with welcoming one individual, or are setting up community groups that enable individuals to come to church, God can do immeasurably more with what we bring.

Chapter 14: Rooted in Community

'Just as a body, though one, has many parts, but all its many parts form one body, so it is with Christ. For we were all baptized by one Spirit so as to form one body—whether Jews or Gentiles, slave or free—and we were all given the one Spirit to drink. Even so the body is not made up of one part but of many. Now if the foot should say, "Because I am not a hand, I do not belong to the body," it would not for that reason stop being part of the body. And if the ear should say, "Because I am not an eye, I do not belong to the body," it would not for that reason stop being part of the body. If the whole body were an eye, where would the sense of hearing be? If the whole body were an ear, where would the sense of smell be? But in fact God has placed the parts in the body, every one of them, just as he wanted them to be. If they were all one part, where would the body be? As it is, there are many parts, but one body.
The eye cannot say to the hand, "I don't need you!" And the head cannot say to the feet, "I don't need you!" On the contrary, those parts of the body that seem to be weaker are indispensable, and the parts that we think are less honourable we treat with special honour. And the parts that are unpresentable are treated with special modesty, while our presentable parts need no special treatment. But God has put

the body together, giving greater honour to the parts that lacked it, so that there should be no division in the body, but that its parts should have equal concern for each other. If one part suffers, every part suffers with it; if one part is honoured, every part rejoices with it. Now you are the body of Christ, and each one of you is a part of it.'
(1 Corinthians 12: 12-31)

We are the body of Christ and each one of us is a part of that body. God calls us to be in a community in which we all work together. As Paul says in this passage, no one part of the body can work in isolation. It is not healthy to have a community full of only one part of the body. When we choose to welcome individuals who the world see as less important, we are stepping further into this picture of a body in which every part is recognised as unique and significant. When we work fully together as a community we can more easily enable everyone to be a part of what we are doing. We are then stepping further towards the call Jesus gives us to, *'Go and make disciples of all nations'* (Matthew 28:20) – for all people to have the opportunity to hear about and grow in relationship with God.

The most common difficulty that people approach me with as head of accessibility for New Wine is: 'What do I do with the individual I have who has additional needs and cannot participate in the same way as everyone else?' Sadly, I find that most people's natural reaction is to try and create something separate; to try to sideline the individual to another room, at the back, or somewhere where it is easier to engage them in something different to everyone else. I would suggest that this is not the best way to start. The more we can create accessibility as part of our community and culture, the more we are reflecting the body of Christ as God intended it.

There will be times when we get it wrong. I was a respite carer within a care home for children and young people with additional needs whilst I was at uni. There was one morning where I was looking after an older teenager called Ollie. Ollie was very slim, but much much taller than me, and could have very easily hurt me if he'd wanted to. Ollie has a diagnosis of autism. I was getting Ollie ready to go to school and I had got him dressed into his uniform. I then checked his school bag to make sure he had everything he needed. On checking, I noticed he had a social story (written information which includes a picture and simple sentences) about how it was a non-uniform day that day. I had a dilemma and wondered what to do. If Ollie turned up at school and all his friends were not in uniform, that would be really difficult for him. I decided to sit down with Ollie and talk through the social story, and to then quickly help him change into his own clothes before his bus arrived. Ollie thought he was ready for the morning and was happily doing a puzzle waiting for his bus. Reading the social story and saying that we would change his clothes did not go down well, as I'd suspected. Ollie became very agitated and upset. He towered over me, waving his arms close to my face and shouting at me. It took what felt like a long time for someone to come and help me, but they did. In that moment I could not support Ollie on my own. I needed people who had additional training and knew what they were doing to come alongside me and help Ollie calm down. Ollie was then able to change into his own clothes and head to school.

In that moment I had been afraid that Ollie was going to hit me. I was not big enough to stop him and I could not easily move away. I was intimidated, but unable to do anything until someone came to help me. I felt upset that I had caused Ollie's distress because I did not check his school bag before I'd got him up and dressed. There will be moments where this kind of thing happens. We will all have times where we try to prepare to do things well but they go wrong. If we do this in community, with people around us who can step in to help, then we can more easily support each other and enable everyone to participate. The more we practice doing accessibility together the easier it will become. We will build on our ability to work together and support each other in situations that might be challenging. We will have more wisdom as to when we need to step in and support those in our community.

When we respond together we are also able to be more welcoming. It is really important not just to welcome individuals with additional needs, but their carers and families as well. During New Wine's United summer gatherings we have a venue called *Breathe*. This venue is for parents and carers of individuals with additional needs. The idea is to give parents and carers the opportunity to have space to breathe; space to be themselves and not just be known as 'Tommy's mum' or 'Susie's dad'. Breathe is a place where parents and carers can journey through their experiences together in a safe place, build relationship with one another and connect with God afresh. Through Breathe we have many stories of parents who have had the opportunity to share both celebrations and challenges together. There are stories of couples being able to receive prayer and the opportunity to process things in their marriages, where they have been under extra stress because of caring for a child with significant additional needs. We have had the chance to explore and celebrate with parents and carers who God has called *them* to be, and talk about the unique value and gifting he sees in them and their child. We have had discussions about what it is like to have hopes for an individual with additional needs and to have the disappointment of some of these hopes not coming to fruition. We have listened as parents have wrestled with the 'now and not yet' of God's kingdom and the question of healing. Breathe has enabled families to have the opportunity to reconnect with God in the midst of the ups and downs of being parents and carers of individuals with additional needs. Through Breathe people have had a fresh realisation of the church community they are a part of. They know that they are a valued and important part of the body of Christ and that they can walk and be in community with the people around them.

Within your church community, as you develop accessibility ministry, it can be important to recognise the experience of parents and carers as they support the individuals they love in day to day life. This might start with enabling the parents and carers to also be a part of the community. If an individual has additional needs, often the parents or carers cannot attend other church events as they will at home caring for the individual in their family. By offering to support or care for an individual with additional needs, other members of the family may have more opportunity to go to church events and feel a part of the church family. Often individuals with additional needs and their families can feel like they are on the edges of society; they can feel pushed to one side, or that they are more of a challenge to the people around them. As a church community we can help to shift this perception and stand against what the world thinks. We can do this by being intentional about the way in which we invite people for dinner or lunch after church, the way that we spend time with people and get to know them.

As a church community, if we start to enable families of individuals with additional needs to be a part of our church communities we start to break a possible sense of isolation. As we come alongside those who may not otherwise not be part of a church, there is a chance that they do not have many other community supports in place. Many churches have stories of individuals and their families finding a welcome and a community they didn't have before they started going along to church. Being able to do welcome well can make a really big difference to families. I've heard stories from several families who feel like they are not welcome in their churches, who are told they are too noisy, or that their child's behaviour is too bad, so they cannot physically come in the building. As we challenge this and practically put support in place as a community, we can turn a sense of rejection into a deep knowledge of acceptance which reflects God's kingdom.

When we are thinking about families of individuals with additional needs, we can also consider how we are supporting siblings as well as parents and carers. As a charity, one of the aims of Growing Hope is for families to grow relationally stronger and deeper. We recognise that supporting family members is as important as supporting a child or young person. We are running parenting courses for parents of children and young people with additional needs in order that parents have the opportunity to be supported in their parenting. We have also set up a siblings group for siblings of children with additional needs in a local primary school. We recognise that siblings of individuals with additional needs can often feel like they are responsible for their sibling or that they are always having to let their sibling go first. There are both positive and negative experiences that children may have as siblings of individuals with additional needs. Sibling groups enable the opportunity for children to share and process their experiences with each other. These groups are also enabling siblings to learn more about the additional needs that their siblings have in order that they can understand more of why they might do things in a certain way.

The idea for running siblings groups came from doing this at the United summer gathering as part of Our Place. We run one siblings session each year in which we find that siblings really benefit from the opportunity to share their experiences with each other. We have siblings who have built relationships and friendships with other siblings which have lasted throughout the year.

Another part of Growing Hope is to provide training for schools in order that they can more easily support and come alongside children with additional needs. This training is important because it enables those in community around the child and family to more easily love and support them in their day to day. The more of the local community who can learn and understand what additional needs are and how to support individuals, the more we will start to see a shift in culture in which every individual is valued for who they are and who God has made them to be.

Being community together is mainly about seeing and recognising this value. If we ask God to give us his eyes to see, and we recognise the value that he has placed on every single individual, we will learn to more naturally respond as a church community. If we enable an adult with a learning disability to be a part of the church café, or tea and coffee team, we are recognising a gift they have to welcome and host others and enabling them to be a part of a team as they do that. This helps to build community and helps individuals to not see an adult with additional needs as someone who needs looking after, but as someone who is part of the family. In the Ephesian's 3 passage Paul talks about being *rooted and established* in God's love. If, as God's people, we have our roots deep in God's love we will more easily be able to see the love and value he has for everyone in our communities.

As part of being a community we can therefore choose to love well and put healthy boundaries in place in order that as a community we can create a culture of care in which everyone is part of family together. If everyone has a healthy rhythm of being able to use their gifts and skills, of being able to ask for help when they need it, of being able to come alongside or encourage others in their own unique way, we can create a community which everyone feels a part of. Being rooted in community starts with being rooted in God's love. As we grasp more of his love for us as individuals, and for the people around us, the more each and every individual can turn their eyes outwards from themselves to the community around them.

This week you could take a practical step towards creating more of a sense of community for an individual with additional needs in your church. This could be offering to babysit for a parent, inviting a person over for a meal, encouraging someone in the gifts you see that God has put in them, or choosing to have a conversation and say hello to someone who you might not normally chat to. Whatever you're thinking of doing, why not write it down now as a reminder to yourself to take action.

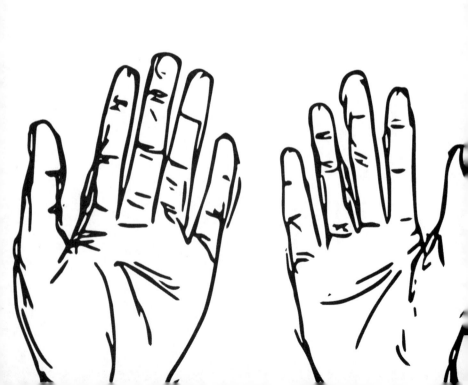

Chapter 15: Starting With Mustard Seeds

'And when they came to the crowd, a man came up to him and, kneeling before him, said, "Lord, have mercy on my son, for he has seizures and he suffers terribly. For often he falls into the fire, and often into the water. And I brought him to your disciples, and they could not heal him." And Jesus answered, "O faithless and twisted generation, how long am I to be with you? How long am I to bear with you? Bring him here to me." And Jesus rebuked the demon, and it came out of him, and the boy was healed instantly. Then the disciples came to Jesus privately and said, "Why could we not cast it out?" He said to them, "Because of your little faith. For truly, I say to you, if you have faith like a grain of mustard seed, you will say to this mountain, 'Move from here to there', and it will move, and nothing will be impossible for you."'
(Matthew 17:14-20)

You are probably familiar with this passage in which Jesus tells the disciples that faith as small as a mustard seed can move mountains. As we come to the end of this book, I wonder what that mustard seed might look like for you? What do you have faith to see happen within your church community? What has

God placed in your heart that you are going to step out with from here?

Perhaps you've already acted upon that spark we talked about at the beginning, or perhaps you haven't yet. If we choose to make small changes we can start to see mountains moved.

I'm always encouraged by the stories of small changes made within children's groups and churches and the difference that they make. Following a training session about creating a more accessible church, one leader in a church handed something to fiddle with to Meg, who was struggling to concentrate. Meg was so appreciative that it had been recognised that she was finding it difficult, and that it might help if she had something in her hands. Meg was then able to get herself to that 'just right' level where she could focus. She went up to the leader and said 'Thank you for giving me this, I don't need it now.' Meg had been enabled to use equipment when she needed it in a way that was comfortable and supportive.

In the same church there was a little boy called Luke who was struggling to participate in the sessions because it was too noisy. The children's leaders tried giving Luke ear defenders to use, which he wasn't keen on initially, but towards the end of the session he asked for them. Since then it has really enabled Luke to join in, and he asks for the ear defenders when he needs them. The leaders feel that it has really helped and Luke's parents are looking into buying some of his own.

In another church there is a story from a children's pastor of a five-year old called Danny who has significant additional needs. When Danny's family were coming along to church they were in the middle of trying to work out how he could be best supported in the education system. The leaders therefore found that they were journeying with the parents and the family as they discovered what Danny's needs were. Danny has complicated medical needs which include epilepsy and each time Danny had a seizure his needs would become more profound and his behaviour would change. The team therefore had to learn how to support Danny with his changing behaviour and needs each week. This led to the set up of a quiet corner at the back of the kids room, so that Danny could be supported to retreat there if he was struggling with a part of the programme. As the team got to know Danny more, the additional needs ministry within the church grew. Other families with children with additional needs started coming along. The kids pastor then developed a team to enable children with additional needs to be included on a Sunday. For the kids pastor, coming alongside Danny's mother was a precious relationship in which she discovered what it was like to walk with a parent who was coming into the full knowledge of her son's needs. The kid's pastor said that there were many hiccups along the way, but through Danny, and then others, the team's hearts were changed and eyes opened to doing things in a slightly different way.

Small changes can also be made within adult ministry that enable adults to be able to join in. One example is printing out some large-print copies of the worship songs in order that adults with visual difficulties can read and then participate in the singing. This can make a really big difference to adults who can otherwise be lost as to what is happening in the worship.

So often, the changes we can make only take a small amount of resource, or involve using something already available to us. Most churches have a printer and the song words – that makes sorting out large-print song words really easy. I wonder what you have available to you? What gifts, skills and resources do you already have and could use to create a greater level of accessibility where you are? At KXC (King's Cross Church), a question we often take time to ask while listening to God is 'What's in your hands?' This is a question that carries massive power and helps us realise the resources available to us and the way that God can move in our churches and communities. We often hear the story of Tearfund going to a community and asking them 'What's in your hands?' A combination of events then led to that community creating thriving ponds with fish they could sell, using land which was previously swamp land and regarded as useless. The simple question of looking at what was already available to them helped transform a community and lift them out of poverty.

It was that question, *what's in your hands?* that led me to set up Growing Hope. Growing Hope has a vision to see twenty free therapy clinics for children and young people with additional needs run through local churches by 2030. Growing Hope King's Cross is the first clinic to be set up, which is where I work. We aim to grow hope for every child to reach their developmental potential (through free therapy clinics), hope for families to grow relationally stronger and deeper (through parenting courses, sibling groups and family activities), and hope in Jesus (through being openly Christian and offering to pray for individuals who come to the clinic). The idea to start Growing Hope came from seeing the church respond to health needs whilst I was on short trips to Thailand and India, volunteering as a children's occupational therapist. I had the realisation that the church in the UK has so many healthcare professionals within our churches who work with health services, yet there is an increasing difficulty in being able to talk about faith and the hope that Jesus brings. I had a dream that perhaps I could start something similar to what I saw in Thailand and India in churches in the UK. I had been working in the NHS and felt the pressure and the stretch on services for families. I had been in private practice and seen families who had bailiffs knocking on their door scraping everything together to pay for therapy, because they knew that their son benefitted from it. There are several children and young people with additional needs (and adults) who do not get the therapy they need, or would benefit from, to support their everyday lives. One Sunday, during worship, I had a picture of what it would look like to provide therapy for free to these families to help bridge the gap for the stretched NHS services. Then Pete Hughes spoke out that very challenge: *what's in your hands?* What are you holding? What dreams, skills and visions has God put in your heart that you could see come to fruition? In that moment I knew I needed to push the door, to speak out what was in my hands, and talk about the dream I had and to see what happened.

Two years on from the initial conversation I had with Pete about that dream, we are a few months into having set up Growing Hope. We are seeing families in the local area who have children with additional needs have the opportunity to receive therapy and also hear about Jesus. We have groups for siblings of children with additional needs and parenting courses set up, and we have had the opportunity to pray for families. It is such an honour to have been supported by Pete and KXC, my incredible trustees and all the amazing friends, family and others who have given to enable the charity to run.

Jesus promises that faith as small as a mustard seed can move mountains. Let's choose to step out in faith with the things that God has put in our hands. Whether they are small or big God can use them to make a difference within our church communities. As we do this we will start to see transformation across the land in which more and more individuals, no matter whether they have additional needs or not, will know, deep down, God's love which surpasses knowledge.

Appendix 1
Additional needs that you may come across

This is by no means an exhaustive list or a fully expanded description of each additional need. Every individual is *'fearfully and wonderfully made'* (Psalm 139). We are all unique and made in God's image. We should first look to the individual rather than to their disability or need. This list is here to try and be a helpful starting point. It looks at each additional need with a broad brush stroke. Almost 100% of the time an individual that you come across will not exactly meet the description here. Please use this list to help you gain a broad understanding, rather than to categorise and rigidly understand and respond to an individual's needs.

Anxiety & Depression
We all have times where we will feel anxious or low, but anxiety disorders and depression involve a persistent presence of symptoms. Individuals with anxiety feel anxious to the extent that it impacts their daily life. This can have a range of symptoms including restlessness, dread, dizziness and heart palpitations. Individuals with depression can have persistent low mood and feelings of hopelessness – which could, at times, lead to being suicidal, tearfulness and tiredness. There is often some overlap in anxiety and depression symptoms.

Attachment Disorder
This can occur following difficulty with gaining a secure bond with our primary caregiver. There are two main types of attachment disorder: an inhibited form, where an individual does not expect care or comfort, and a disinhibited form which can result in excessive overfamiliarity, even with strangers.

Attention Deficit and Hyperactivity Disorder (ADHD)
This is a group of behaviours which normally results in an

individual consistently displaying inattentiveness, hyperactivity and impulsiveness. Individuals with ADHD often particularly benefit from lots of opportunities for movement breaks.

Autism
Individuals with autism primarily have difficulty with the way they communicate with and relate to other people. Autism is a spectrum condition and some individuals will be cognitively very capable and able to live and function independently. Other individuals will have significant needs, may not develop language, and may need support for their whole lives. Individuals with autism will generally also have sensory processing difficulties.

Bipolar Disorder
This is characterised by episodes of extreme mood disturbance, which can sometimes swing. However, individuals can fully recover in between each episode. Episodes can range from extreme highs (mania) to extreme lows (depression). These episodes will often last a period of weeks or months and will impact an individual's behaviour.

Borderline Personality Disorder (BPD)
Is a disorder of mood and how a person interacts with others. It's the most commonly recognised personality disorder. Symptoms include emotional instability, disturbed patterns of thinking, impulsive behaviour and intense but unstable relationships with others.

Cerebral Palsy
Is caused by a lack of oxygen to the developing brain. Individuals with Cerebral Palsy will generally present with a physical disability. This could involve only one limb, part of their body (hemiplegia or diplegia), or all of their body (quadriplegia). Some individuals with Cerebral Palsy will have difficulties with learning and perception, whilst others may not. It is possible for individuals to have high levels of physical disability (which means that they use a wheelchair, may not be able to use their voice to

speak, and may need help with all their personal care) but also be highly intelligent.

Dementia

There are many forms of Dementia. It is rare in individuals under 65 years old. Dementia is a progressive disease of the brain which impacts a variety of brain functions including memory. It also causes an impairment to the ability to function independently. Individuals with dementia often lose their memory gradually and benefit from the opportunity to continue routine activities.

Down's Syndrome

This is caused by an extra 21st chromosome in an individual's cells. Individuals with Down's Syndrome will particularly have low muscle tone (which means they appear more floppy than others), a learning disability (which means learning can take a long time and a lot of repetition is needed) and delayed development of speech and learning to walk. Some individuals will often have associated health conditions involving their sight, hearing and heart.

Dyspraxia/ Developmental Coordination Disorder

Developmental Coordination Disorder (DCD) is an umbrella term which now is used to cover more specific conditions such as Dyspraxia. Dyspraxia is solely about an individual's ability to understand the movement they need to make in order to carry out a task. DCD involves other aspects of motor difficulty such as using two hands together, being able to stabilise joints for movement activities and having strong abdominal muscles. DCD is diagnosed if an individual's motor difficulties impact upon activities they do every day (such as dressing, eating, handwriting) and are significantly below their learning ability.

Drug and Alcohol Addiction

Addiction is defined as not having control over what you are doing to the extent where you take or use something that could be harmful to you. Misuse of drugs and alcohol can have serious psychological and physical effects.

Global Developmental Delay

This explains a delay in children's development. In order to be diagnosed with Global Developmental Delay a child is likely to have delays in their learning development.

Schizophrenia

This is a severe, long term mental health condition where individuals often find it difficult to distinguish their own thoughts and ideas from reality. These difficulties are often described as 'psychosis'.

Sensory Processing Disorder / difficulties

The diagnosis of Sensory Processing Disorder is rarely given in the UK. Several individuals may have sensory processing difficulties that are significant enough to impact their everyday life. Individuals may be hypersensitive to touch to the point that they only eat certain foods and cannot stand their hair being cut or teeth being brushed. They may seek out movement to the extent that they can never sit still. They may be so sensitive to sound that they cannot go into loud or busy places.

Spinal Cord Injuries

These can occur following trauma, disease or infection to the spine. There are different levels of injury which impact different individuals in different ways. The higher up the spine an injury occurs, the greater the level of impairment. Spinal cord injuries can impact how much an individual can move and how much they can feel with different parts of their body. A spinal cord injury in the neck would likely lead to paralysis in all four limbs and an individual needing a lot of support.

Appendix 2
Additional needs form

	Name	
	Date of Birth (if under 18)	
	Contact number	
	Parent/ Carer name and contact number (if applicable)	
	Brief description of needs	
	What am I likely to find difficult in church?	
	What helps me participate?	
	If I am upset how can people help me?	
	What medical needs or allergies do I have?	
	What support do I need with moving, eating, drinking or personal care?	
	Signed by	
	Date	
	I consent for the following (please tick if this is necessary)	o Support with personal care o Support with eating and drinking o Use of suncream/ lotion/ messy play

Appendix 3
All about proprioception

Proprioception (body awareness) is our subconscious awareness of where our body is in space. The more proprioceptive or *heavy work* activities we do, the more regulated we feel. This is because proprioception sends signals to our brain which help to improve our attention and concentration. The more *movement breaks* or physical activities we build into everything we're doing, the more everyone will be enabled to participate. These are some ideas of heavy work movement activities that you could use (some are more appropriate for children, some more for adults).

Dance in worship

Walking like a bear

Stacking chairs

Chair push up

Big hug

Bouncing on a gym ball

Wiping tables

Pushing the wall

Chewy sweet

Walking like a crab

Carrying heavy books

Appendix 4 – Kids ministry session plans

Please feel free to use these plans. They are all based on eight sessions which you could use within one half term. For an idea of how to tell a sensory story see the example in appendix 5. An outline of a session would be shown with a visual schedule and might involve the following: singing, hello time, free play, story, prayer, movement break, making, play, singing, home time.

(**these tables hopefully will fit horizontally one per page or double spread so that it's a quick overview people can work from**)

God made my body

Session	Key message	Movement activity	Multisensory story	Ministry time/ Prayer activity	Making activity
1	Thank you God for my hands	Slow crab walk race (hands and feet on the floor bottom in the air) see who can avoid the sharks and move slowly across the room.	Pieces of a Jenga tower in the story box- everyone can help build a tower together. What do we use our hands for? God has given us our hands to do things. Jesus laid hands on people when he healed them (Luke 4:40).	Prayer button 'Thank you God for my hands'. Lay hands on each child, encourage the children to do this too. If someone does not like the way their hands work see if they would like prayer for healing.	Play with paint and make handprints on pieces of paper. Talk about the things we can do with our hands.
2	Thank you God for my feet	See if everyone can walk along a path made of masking tape on the floor. Follow the leader.	Picture of feet covered in words. Jesus says that his bible is a path for our feet (Psalm 119:105). Have a character who is lost- God shows them the way to go and guides their feet.	Prayer button 'Thank you God for my feet'. If children would like it massage their feet with baby lotion and pray they would always know the direction God is leading them in. If someone doesn't like the way their feet work offer to pray for healing.	Play with clay and make footprints in pieces of clay. Talk about how God takes us where he wants us to go- where do we need God's help?
3	Thank you God for my eyes	The key game, one child sits on a chair blindfolded with keys underneath, they have to point to try and catch the other children who are crawling up to try and steal the keys.	Have a character whose hat has fallen over their head and they can't see where they are going. Jesus helps us to see where we're going, have a torch in the box- he is like a light in the dark (John 1:5).	Prayer button 'Thank you God for my eyes'. Pass around a torch that reminds us how Jesus helps us shine like lights in the darkness. If someone doesn't like the way their eyes work offer to pray for healing.	Use magnifying glasses to look at different things. What can you see around the room? What is God saying through what we can see?
4	Thank you God for my ears	The wiggle song, see if you can freeze when the music stops.	Have a character whose put a headband over their ears so they can't hear. God uses our ears to help us to hear what's going on around us. He talks to us in different ways but sometimes in a whisper. Tell the story	Prayer button 'Thank you God for my ears'. Pass the ear defenders around so everyone can try them- see if that helps hear God whispering. If someone doesn't like the way their	Make shakers with different sounds using different things in them (e.g. beads, pasta, dried peas, rice). Talk about how God likes to talk to us in

#	Theme	Activity	Story / Teaching	Prayer	Exploration / Craft
			of Elijah (1 Kings 19:11-3) use a big piece of card you can flap (wind), tissue paper (fire), cymbals and stamping feet (earthquake) in the story box.	ears work offer to pray for healing.	different ways, we don't always hear him with our ears.
5	Thank you God for my mouth	See how many Maltesers everyone can move from one bowl to another by sucking on a straw.	God has given us an amazing mouth. Have different crunchy snacks in the story box (check what children can have) e.g. breadsticks, carrot, apple, rice cakes. We can taste and see how good God is (Psalm 34:8).	Prayer button "Thank you God for my mouth". Offer another crunchy snack and pray for everyone one at a time. If someone doesn't like the way their mouth works offer to pray for healing.	Make blow paintings where you blow paint with straws. Have hand pumps to squeeze for children who find it difficult. Talk about how we use our mouths. Has God given you special things he wants you to be sharing and saying?
6	Thank you God for my skin	Do a dressing up relay race in two teams.	Have a character who really needs a cuddle. A cuddly heart or toy in the story box. God can speak to us through our skin. He wants us to know we are loved and cared for. Tell the story of Jesus welcoming children, touching them and praying for them (Matthew 19:13-15).	Prayer button "Thank you God for my skin". Spend time with hands open seeing if God speaks to anyone through making their skin feel different. If someone doesn't like the way their skin works offer to pray for healing.	Our skin helps us to be able to tell the difference between things. God made our body and all the different parts. Cut out different fabrics and textures to stick onto a body.
7	Thank you God for my head	Do animal walk races- who can race from one side of the room to the other like a crab, a bear, a snake etc.	Where is your head, head, shoulders knees and toes. Have a character who is really confused. Have some books in the story box, have a short video clip you can play. Sometimes we're confused but God can help us to learn- we might learn through reading, or listening, watching something or feeling something with our bodies. Talk about Jesus discussing things in the temple (Luke 2:41-52).	Prayer button 'Thank you God that you speak to me in my head'. Ask God a question like 'what game do you want to play with me? And why that game? If someone has a headache or thinks there is something wrong with their head offer to pray for healing.	Look at pictures of different things (e.g. family dinner, someone falling over in the playground) talk about big questions. How do they make God feel, what does he say about them? Stick, draw or write about the different pictures.
8	Thank you God for my heart	See who can find heart sweeties in jelly.	Have a character who is feeling sad and then realises Jesus speaks to their heart and loves them. Have a picture of a hug, a wrapped up present and arms wide open in the story box. Talk through the gospel. (John 3:16). God loves us SO much that he sent Jesus. We can be Jesus' friend in our heart.	Prayer button 'Thank you God that I can know you as my friend in my heart'. Spend time lying under a parachute asking God to speak to our hearts. Ask everyone what God said. If someone doesn't like the way their heart works offer to pray for healing.	Play with cornflour and water and see who can make heart shapes. Talk about how God speaks to our heart as well as our head and how much Jesus loves us even when we make mistakes.

God loves everyone

Session	Key message	Movement activity	Multisensory story	Ministry time/ Prayer activity	Making activity
1	God created the world	Digging in a sandpit to build sand castles. Or making things out of clay.	Story box with a torch (light), water spray (waters and heavens), clay/ mud (land and seas), herbs that everyone can hold/ smell/ taste (plants), glow sticks (stars, sun and moon), fish and bird toy (fish and birds), plastic animals (animals on the land), doll (Adam and Eve). God created the world and it was good. (Genesis 1).	Choose something from the story box that you want to say thank you to God for. Prayer button- 'Thank you God that you created the world'.	If you can go on a walk outside and thank God for all the amazing things that he's made. Use some twigs etc. to make a picture with things from outside.
2	God wants all families to know him	Slow crab walk races (hands and feet on the floor bottom in the sky) trying to avoid the sharks across the room.	Story box with a character who could be Abraham, a star, some sand, a map. Tell the story of how God promises Abraham that all families of the earth will be blessed by him. (as many as the stars and sand). Abraham listens to God and goes where he tells him. (Genesis 12)	Prayer button 'Thank you God that you want everyone to be your friend'. Using some playdough make models (or just chat to God while moving the playdough) about all the people in the world he wants to know him.	What does God mean by all families? Who is similar to me? Who is different? Is there someone I can be kind to this week because God wants them to be in his family as much as me? Draw this.
3	We're part of one body	Musical statues, see if you can freeze and make different positions with your body.	Story box with a doll in it. Play Simon Says and see who can touch different parts of their body. Talk about how we're all the body of Christ (1 Corinthians 12:12-27). What would it be like if we were only one part? God has given us all special parts to play.	Prayer button 'Thank you God that I'm part of your body'. Pray that God will show everyone the part they have to play. Using stickers and a doll, stick stickers on the doll to see if God wants to heal a certain part of someone's body or speak to someone who feels like they are this part (you could share this with the wider church).	Paint pictures of our bodies and talk about which part of the body God may have made you to be like. What does God love most about you?
4	All one in Jesus	Animal walk races. See if you can race across the room like different animals (E.g. a crab, a bear, a snake).	Have a character that doesn't want to play with anyone at their new school because they all seem so different to them. Have a long piece of rope or cloth in the story box- see if everyone can hold onto it. Talk about how we are all one in Jesus, we all have things he loves about us and he wants us to be able to celebrate each other. (Galatians 3:28)	Prayer button- 'Thank you God that we're all one in Jesus'. Spend time with one child in the middle asking God what he likes about them, write this down in their prayer book.	Look at magazine pictures or pre cut out pictures of people who might be different to us (e.g. a grown up, a baby, someone from a different country, someone living in poverty). Talk about why they might be different but how in Jesus we are all one.

#	Theme	Game	Story	Prayer	Craft
5	Jesus loves children	Over and Under with a foam ball in two teams.	Have a character who cannot do anything because their mummy doesn't let them (they're too little to pour their drink, to put on their socks). Have some tuna in a Tupperware and some bread the children can share. Tell the story about the boy who shared his lunch (John 6:1-14). Sometimes people do not realise what children have to bring but Jesus always sees what we have and loves us.	Prayer button 'Thank you Jesus that you love me and love that I'm young'. Jump up and do a big high ten when you pray for every child. Speak over them the things that God loves about them.	Draw around each other on big pieces of paper. Talk about how Jesus loves us and wants us to follow him even though we're little. You could discuss Timothy- 1 Timothy 4:12.
6	Jesus loves people no one else liked	Obstacle course, see who can create the best obstacle course. (If you can do it outside you could do it with carrying a cup of water).	Story box with a toy character who is sad because everyone says they don't like them and no one has invited them to their party. Jesus knew what it was like. Have two scarves in the box so someone can dress up as the Samaritan woman by the well and someone as Jesus. No one liked the woman but Jesus showed her he loved her and enabled her to know she could be friends with the people she lived with (John 4:1-42).	Prayer button 'Thank you Jesus that you love people no one else likes'. Spend some time lying down (put some quiet music on). Tell Jesus about someone you maybe don't like. Ask Jesus what he wants to say to them, talk to the children/ write down what is said.	Have a big groundsheet or builders tray with shaving foam in it. Make pictures or write words and rub them out. Talk about whether there are people that you don't like, what is God asking us to do? How can we learn from Jesus?
7	Jesus always brings hope	Play with some mud, sand and straw, see who can build a house like the houses in Jesus' time. (or use some lego/ duplo).	Story box with a character who is sad because they always bump into things. Jesus gives them hope. Story box with a mat, straw. Tell the story of the man lowered through the roof. Jesus loves him so much that he gives him hope first by forgiving him and becoming his friend and then by healing him. (Luke 5:17-24).	Prayer button 'Thank you Jesus that you bring hope.' See if there's anyone that would like God to heal something for them? Pray for healing. Use some clay and either mould it into something or just hold it as you chat to God.	Draw with felt tips on some balloons the things you want to say thank you to God for because he gives you hope. Blow these up and play with them/ have a disco.
8	Jesus shows us how to love others	Play Captains coming. See if children can 'man the lifeboats' together with everyone.	Have a character who is really good at loving other people (have them giving someone a big hug, encouraging someone, helping a friend in the playground). Talk about what it means to be friends with Jesus. Jesus tells us to tell other people (Matthew 28:20)- how can we do that?	Prayer button 'Thank you Jesus that I can share your love'. Lie under the parachute and spend time listening to God- ask him to put the name of someone in our head he wants us to share him with.	Have cut out symbols of different people e.g. mummy, daddy, granny, grandpa, cousin, friend. Help everyone to choose someone they would like to share Jesus' love with. Pray for that person.

God's treasure (written with Susie Yeates)

For this series each key message has one small object which the children put in a treasure box and build up throughout the sessions. We used wooden boxes from Baker Ross but you could use any kind of box and then give the finished box to the children at the end of the series.

Session	Key message	Movement activity	Multisensory story	Ministry time/ Prayer activity	Making activity
1	Heart- God loves us	Stuck in the mud (arms wide open- talk about how God's love goes wider than we can imagine)	Use a bowl, spoon, flannel, socks, book, picture of a parent giving a child a big hug to talk about how much our Mum and Dad's love us and how much more God loves us. Eat heart shaped sweets (or pieces of apple) and read 1 John 3, Romans 8:38-39.	Singing over you- Zephaniah 3:17. *Singing over us with your love* (Song by KXC). Parachute prayer soaking. Use the prayer button 'Thank-you God that you love me SO much!'	Share examples of times God has shown you he loves you. Use clay either to mould in your hands as you chat or to make a model. Talk about why God sent Jesus, how he shows us how much he loves us. Put a heart in treasure box.
2	Sparkly gems- God thinks we're precious	Find treasure in theraputty or clay (hide small beads in theraputty or a big bit of clay, see if everyone can find the treasure)	Use playdough and ask children to make Moses, a mountain, a group of people, the red sea, pharaoh. Talk through Moses leading the Egyptians out of Egypt, through the red sea, and hearing God say that they are his treasured possession.	Look in the mirror and use the prayer button- 'Thank-you God that you've made me precious'. Help everyone ask God what is the most precious thing about the person you're praying for- write this in prayer books. Jesus has put his treasure in us (2 Corinthians 4:7-11)	Decorate their treasure box or make a bracelet of sparkly treasure. Put a piece of treasure in box. Talk about what God thinks is the most precious thing about you. Talk about what the word treasured means. Why does God call us treasured?
3	Finger print and first letter of name- God made the world and everyone as unique and individual	Musical statues- everyone is unique, can you jump/ hop/ skip/ crawl/ walk like an animal around the room and then freeze?	Use pictures of different body parts in the story box and have a dolly that you can look at all their body parts. Talk about 1 Corinthians 12 and how we all have a part to play. See who can touch the body part you hold a picture up of first.	Pray for each other in pairs. Talk through it- find a partner, ask your partner what they would like prayer for, pray for your partner that they would know that God has made them a part of his body, swap. Write down in prayer journals any words/ pics. Prayer button- 'Thank you God that you've made me unique'	Make finger prints on small bit of card for treasure box. Talk about why God made us unique. What does your name mean? What would happen if we were all the same?
4	Star- shine like stars in the darkness	Glow stick disco. Turn the lights off and do some jumping, moving and dancing with a glow stick disco.	Have a torch and a big blanket in the story box. Put the blanket over everyone's heads or turn the lights off and look at the light. You always notice the light in the darkness. Jesus came as a light in the world (John 8:12), he fills us with his light so we can shine in the darkness (Philippians 2:15).	Prayer button- "Thank you God that you shine brightly in me'. Pray that God would show each child the way that they shine. Draw pictures in prayer journals. Ask God to put one friend in our head he wants us to shine to.	Use glitter glue and black paper to draw pictures of light shining in the darkness. Talk about who God wants to shine to? And where abouts e.g. at school, swimming, home, bedtime etc. Put star into treasure boxes.

5	Magnifying glass- I know everything about you	Treasure hunt, who can crawl around the room and find all the puzzle pieces (cut up picture of grass). How many pieces of grass are there? God knows everything about us.	Props in the box for each section of the psalm, ask children to get them out and then talk it through. Psalm 139:1-18 (toy chair, picture of a path, needle and thread, toy car/ aeroplane, torch, baby doll, sand).	Prayer button- 'Thank you God you know everything about me' Write or talk out psalm 139 in their own words. Spend time quietly reading back what they've written and asking God what he wants to say.	Put a magnifying glass into the treasure box. Spend time writing out or drawing what the children thought or said about psalm 139 so that they can take it home.
6	Speech bubble (make out of card)- We're significant and called	Animal walks- see if you can do animal walk races across the room (crab, bear, snake etc.).	Talk through Esther story, act it out (have different costumes in the story box). God used Esther to save his people. Talk about Jeremiah 29:11 God has plans for us.	Prayer button- 'Thank you God that I'm significant and called by you'. In a group sit someone in the middle and ask God to show us what he loves about us	Decorate your speech bubble. What does God want to say to you? Ask God if there's something that he's calling you to.
7	Book-We're part of a bigger story	Scooter board relay. See if two teams can go across the room on scooter boards on their tummies.	In the story box have zoomed in pictures, see if the children can look at them and guess what it is. We're all part of a bigger story of God's plan. Talk about the old and the new testament and give an overview of how Jesus is coming. Talk about the dream that God gives Daniel (just after God has rescued him from the lions) and how he's showing Daniel the bigger story (Daniel 7:13-14)	Prayer button- 'Thank you God that we're part of a bigger story'. Use bubbles and blow and pop them to say thank you to God for all the things that we can think of which mean we're part of his story.	Make a little book- start a story and don't finish it. Chat about What is the bigger story? Why did God make a story with us in it? What's God's story in our lives- make a timeline of our own lives.
8	Different coloured beads-It's okay that we're different	Jumping game (jumping bean, runner bean, broad bean)	In the story box have pictures of different people (e.g. a granny, a baby, the tallest man in the world etc). Talk about how it doesn't matter whether we're big, small, young, old, tall etc. Tell the story of Timothy (1 Timothy 4:12) and how God used him Give and example of how God has used you in your life even though we've been small. Talk about people you know who are different who God has used.	Prayer button- 'Thank you God that it's okay that we're all different'. Give everyone a piece of a puzzle that they can add to a big puzzle during prayer- we are all loved and part of God's family even though we're all different.	Make a bracelet of different kind of beads. Whilst doing that talk about why God make us different? Give the opportunity to talk about additional needs if it comes up and talk about how it's okay to be different.

A King is born (run up to Christmas)

Session	Key message	Movement activity	Multisensory story	Ministry time/ Prayer activity	Making activity
1	Jesus is our King	Crab football, who can walk like a crab and kick a football into a goal.	Story box- have a doll (baby Jesus), a small cross, a crown, and a light. Talk about how Jesus came as a baby but he is our King. He grew up, died on the cross and came back to life. He takes all the dark and not nice things so that we can be friends with God. Because he's a King we're his princess and princess. (John 3:16).	Prayer button- 'Thank you Jesus that you're my king'. Wear the crown from the story box. Lay hands and pray for each child. Spend time lying down and listening to what God is saying- write this into prayer books.	Make crowns to remind us that Jesus is our King and we're his princes and princess'. Talk about why Jesus came as a baby. Talk about how he was a very different king to the other kings.
2	Mary knew Jesus would be King	Find pieces of treasure in theraputty.	Story box- a scarf for Mary, a white smock/ wings for an angel. Act out the story of the angel visiting Mary and her saying 'may it be as God has said' (Luke 1:26-38).	Prayer button – 'Thank you that you came as a baby Jesus'. Later on in the story Mary ponders everything, can we sit quietly and listen to what God is saying to us like Mary did?	Do some drawing in cornflour and water. Has anyone ever seen an angel? Has God told you amazing things? What must it have been like for Mary to know baby Jesus would be a king?
3	Joseph knew Jesus would be king	Musical statues, who can freeze with their hands like a crown on their head.	Have a character who is asleep and try not to wake them. Story box- Cotton wool to remind everyone of dreams- you could pretend to be asleep). Tell the story of God talking to Joseph about Jesus as King in a dream (Matthew 1:18-25).	Prayer button – 'Thank you Jesus that you speak in dreams'. See if we can whisper into our hands what we want to say to God.	Use some cotton wool to plant some cress seeds. Talk about how God had given Joseph a dream about Jesus and he knew that as he grew up (just like the cress grows) he would become a king.
4	The shepherds knew Jesus would be king	The Jumping Bean game (who can be a jumping bean, a broad bean, a runner bean).	Have some sheep, a torch, a white smock/ wings in the story box. Have a character who is a bit silly and has lost their sheep. ask the children to help find the sheep. Talk about what it was like to be a shepherd (how they're often looked down upon as a bit silly) and how the shepherds come to know Jesus would be king. (Luke 2:8-20)	Prayer button- 'Thank you God that you wanted everyone to know when Jesus was born'. Blow bubbles and pop them as you say thank you prayers for Jesus being born and that he wants to show everyone he's king.	Have some black paper and glitter pens, make pictures or play with the glitter using fingers in the paint and onto the paper. Talk about how amazing it must have been for God to talk like that. What's God saying to you?

5	Herod knew Jesus would be king	Animal walk races (see if you can race like a crab, bear, snake etc.)	Have a character who is feeling cross because they are the fastest runner but someone has just joined school who might be faster. Talk about how it feels when someone might want to take our job or something we like doing. Have a crown for Herod in the story box and some cloaks for the wisemen, tell the story and help the children act out what happens for Herod (Matthew 2:1-18).	Prayer button- 'Thank you Jesus that you are king of everything'. Do a big thumbs up or high five as you pray for each child. No king is better than Jesus and we can be his friend.	Have some pictures of lots of different things in the world and things other people are good at (e.g. running, jumping, a smart business man, a leader, a tall building). Talk about how Jesus is king over everything, stick some pictures down and write something along the lines of 'Thank you Jesus that you are king of everything.'
6	The wisemen knew Jesus would be king	Treasure hunt to find the stars like the wisemen were following the star (hide some low and some high).	In the story box have a telescope, some different essential oils that the children can smell for frankincense and mhyr, paint a block gold to show them gold. Talk about how the wisemen were not Jewish people- they did not know the story but they heard God speak to them and knew that Jesus would be king (Matthew 2:1-18).	Prayer button- 'Thank you Jesus that you showed the wisemen were you were'. Look through a telescope like the wisemen might have done.	Make some telescopes and talk about how God showed the wisemen about Jesus being King even though they did not know the story. Talk about who else Jesus might want to know about him.
7	Jesus is a light to the world	Jumping and dancing to a song like 'Shine'	In the story box have a blanket and a torch, look at how you can see the torch light most easily when it's dark under the blanket. Jesus came as a light in the world. Draw on a white t-shirt with washable marker and wash it off. Talk about what Jesus does as a light in the world (John 1:5). Talk about how we can also be lights for him.	Prayer button – 'Thank you Jesus that you shine in me as a light to the world'. Turn off the lights or put a torch under a blanket as you pray.	Make some lanterns with a glowstick or a tea light to light at home. Talk about how we can be lights to people around us who don't know Jesus yet.
8	Lets celebrate Jesus is king	Disco, maybe turn the lights off and play different party games as you celebrate	In the story box have a toy character who is having a party to celebrate their birthday. Have a candle and a birthday cake. Celebrate that Jesus was born and talk about what that means for us because he is our king (Luke 2:4-7).	Prayer button – 'Thank you Jesus that you are King!'. Blow a party blower or hold a balloon or throw the balloon in the sky.	Party games, decorate party hats or gingerbread men as you celebrate that Jesus is King. Talk about what that means for our lives.

Appendix 5
Sensory story example

This is an example of a sensory story and how I would tell it to anyone age 0-11 years to give an idea of how to apply the notes in the tables in Appendix 4.

God made my body session 1 – Thank you God for my hands

Hello, who is ready for our story? (Children will be sitting on fabric squares, will have a wobble cushion if they need it and will have been given a breadstick). Who can show me their hands? Who is holding their breadstick? Let's have a look at what's in my story box (whisper excitedly and choose a child to come and pick out something). Look, it's 'Mr Gorilla' (cuddly toy used for stories). Mr Gorilla can use his hands to do things. What does he do? He can eat a banana. Who can pretend to eat a banana? Do you know what? God gives us our hands so that we can do things.

In the Bible do you know what it says? Who can come and look in my box for a clue? (Have a child come and get a Calpol spoon). When do we have Calpol? When we're poorly. There's a time in the Bible where Jesus goes to a place called Capernaum. He goes to Simon's house and his mother in law is poorly. Jesus heals her and makes her better.

It then says that lots of people come who are poorly. Jesus lays his hands on them and prays for them. Who knows what that means? It means that Jesus put his hand on them (show the children on Mr Gorilla) and prays, and because God is a powerful God he healed them. God could heal them even if

Jesus didn't put his hand on them, but he chose to put his hand on them.

Sometimes in the Bible Jesus chooses to put his hands on people who would not normally be touched because they were poorly. By touching people Jesus is showing that he loves them, that they're welcome and can be part of community. Who knows what community means? *All the people together in one place.*

Who wants to see what else is in our story box? (Choose a child initially who is struggling to focus). A block! Lots of blocks. Shall we give one to everyone? God gives us our hands and our bodies so that we can use them. Let's see if we can use our hands to build a tower all together. Let's say thank you to God for giving us hands that we can use to make things. (Ask a child to find the prayer button from the box). When we pray for each person maybe we could put our hands on them like Jesus did (encourage children to have a go when they're praying).

Appendix 6 – Older youth/ adult bible study discussion and plan

The idea is that these plans can be used with a mainstream youth group or adult small group but will enable individuals with learning disabilities or other additional needs to more easily participate alongside everyone else. To create more plans you could look at the ideas in appendix 4 and adapt these for youth and adults.

Sharing Jesus with my friends

Session	Key message	Bible passage	Multisensory aspect	Discussion	Ministry time/ Prayer activity
1	We can live in relationship with Jesus	Romans 6:1-11	Have some cut out people in white and black paper- use these to talk through how our old self can be set free from sin and how we can live as our new self.	What does this mean for us? How do we personally relate to Jesus?	Talk to Jesus by telling him things and asking questions. E.g. tell God what you had for breakfast, what you did today. Ask God if he could take you to one place right now where would it be and why? Put on some quiet music and spend time listening to him.
2	Why did Jesus die?	Matthew 20:18-19 Luke 23: 46-47	Have some nails and hold them to think about the weight of what happened on the cross. Watch a video clip of what happened or hammer the nails into a piece of wood and think about the extent of what Jesus did.	Have different objects in the room which help to reflect on life which can be turned in on itself (a definition of sin). Money, nice things, a dairy, a pen, a book, a football. Pick up an object and talk about what it looks like to turn that around and give it to Jesus.	Pick up a nail and hammer it into the wood or write/ draw what you want to say sorry to God about and pin that onto the nail on the cross.
3	Why did Jesus come back to life?	Mark 16: 5-6 Luke 24: 5-7 5	Watch a video re-enactment of the tomb being empty and Jesus coming back to life. Close your eyes and try and picture what it might have been like in the garden. Use essential oil that the grave clothes may have smelt of, grass that the garden may have smelt off.	We have a powerful God. What are the things that challenge us most about the resurrection? Have pictures of the empty grave, the curtain torn in two, the grave clothes, the woman seeing first. Pick a picture and talk about why it speaks to you.	Looking at the pictures ask God to give you a fresh revelation of the resurrection and what it means for you and your life.
4	Go and make disciples	Matthew 28:16-20	Have photos of people who are different to the group e.g. younger, older, with and without different needs. Use these to talk about how Gods heart is for all people to come to know him.	What is a disciple? What does it mean? Look at the photos- Gods heart is for all people.	Use paint to make thumb prints, talk about how God has created us uniquely and has called us to go and make disciples. What does that look like for us in our context? Pray for each individual and ask God to show them who he is calling them to share Jesus with.

#	Theme	Scripture	Activity	Reflection / Questions	Prayer Activity
5	Sharing Jesus close to home	Acts 2:42-47	Share a meal with joy and generosity. Talk about what it might have been like for the acts community. Perhaps eat a nice cake together if you don't normally eat meals.	What do they mean by community? (show different pictures of work community, family, church community, small numbers, large numbers). Pick one and discuss why you think that might represent the acts community.	Pray that God would give boldness to share like the Acts community where God added to their number each day. Write or draw the name of someone you want to pray for on a luggage tag- take it home to pray for them each day the following week and to be bold in having conversations.
6	Sharing Jesus far away	Acts 16:6-9	Have a modern map and reflect on how God sends people far away. Find Macedonia (North of Greece) on the map.	What would it be like to have a vision in the middle of the night?	Stick stickers on a map as to places you feel called to pray for or perhaps even to go. What about places you're going on holiday, are there people God wants you to talk to there?
7	Jesus is with me when I'm afraid	Acts 4:23-31	To go with prayer activity- have some fresh grass or herbs and some glasses of water. Drink the water and close your eyes and smell the herbs or grass, picture what it would have been like to lay down with Jesus. When we're afraid he is with us.	God is with us and draws us close when we're afraid of speaking his name. What does that look like in our workplaces? What does it mean that everything is the Lord's? How do we see him stretching out his hand to heal today?	Read psalm 23 out loud a few times, print out a picture and reflect on walking through a dark valley. Are there times where we feel like we're afraid and walking through a valley? We can know God with us in those times.
8	Letting Jesus be in everything I do	Acts 3:1-16	Have a picture of a temple to look at and a watch. Read through the passage, think about how it was a daily place to go for Peter and John and yet they took the time to stop and listen to what God was doing.	How do we share Jesus in our everyday? Perhaps draw out or write your normal weekly pattern. How do you let Jesus in to everything that you're doing?	Look at the schedule you've drawn or written, ask God to highlight one part of that that he wants you to let him into more. Write down what you feel God is saying.

God makes me brave

Session	Key message	Bible passage	Multisensory aspect	Discussion	Ministry time/ Prayer activity
1	I can have relationship with God	John 3:16	Watch a video clip which summarises the gospel narrative. Sit for a minute to reflect on the love that God has, have a bucket of water, a jug of water and a tray and pour the water in until it's overflowing. Reflect on God's love which knows no boundaries (Romans 8).	Everyone may already know they can have relationship with Jesus but take time to reflect on this again. What best sums up your relationship (use a picture of different characters in different place and ask people to identify and then discuss where they feel they are).	Using the picture in which everyone has identified their relationship with God spend time praying and reflecting on what God is saying. Where does he want you to get to, could you draw a new picture of what he is saying to you. Lay hands on each person and pray and speak over them what you feel God is saying in this season.
2	God is powerful	Exodus 3	Could you have a tray of sand people could stand in? twigs that people can hold to think about the fire not burning the wood, perhaps light a candle or a fire to look at the fire. What would it have been like to hear God's voice speak?	God is all knowing and all powerful, he speaks to Moses where he's at. When in your life has God spoken to you most powerfully (have pictures to think about different lifestages which individuals can choose to help them communicate- e.g. as a child, teenager, young adult, family, older adult etc, at a conference, in nature, at work etc.).	What does it mean for us today? Take off your shoes to remind yourselves that you're standing on God's holy ground. Perhaps put some music on in the background and spend time listening to what God might be saying to you. How we will act differently from now? Take a twig home to remember what God said- you could perhaps write this onto your twig.
3	God is a rescuer	Exodus 14:19-31	Use some clay to model the story- think about the scale of the sea compared to thousands of Israelites (use little balls for people). Use this to reflect on the way God rescues his people as you read the passage.	Read the passage a couple of times. What would it have felt like for the Israelites in the sea? For Moses before the sea parts? For Pharaoh? Would the Israelites have needed courage to walk through- how does God give them that?	What is our response? How have we seen God be faithful to what he's said and given us courage in a moment? Use some of the clay and remodel it (either into something or just hold it in your hands) as you reflect on the courage God gives us in his faithfulness to rescue. Are there people around you God wants to rescue?
4	God is in the cloud and the fire	Exodus 13:17-22	Light a fire, maybe watch a video of thick cloud. Reflect on the powerful and tangible way that God was guiding and speaking.	Have a few different maps, discuss what it's like being able to know the direction that we're going in. How does that feel in our own lives? God speaks to us powerfully and makes us brave by guiding us in the way he wants us to go.	Spend time worshipping God together, ask him to move powerfully and reveal himself to you like he did to the Israelites. Spend time praying for each individual, particularly those that feel like they need God to guide them right now.

#	Title	Reference		
5	God makes me brave	Joshua 1:1-9	Have a piece of black cloth or an item of black clothing. Talk about what it can feel like when someone dies. Look at a photo of the river Jordan- have an idea of how many times the room you're in wide it is.	Have some photos of possible dream locations and ask people to choose one- what does it feel like to have something that you've been longing for and promised ahead of you. What about in the face of someone having died and of feeling responsible? How would Joshua have felt with that command to be bold and courageous?	Have some paint and blank pieces of paper, spend time praying and ask God to show you where in your life he's asking you to be bold and courageous. You might want to paint a picture, to write a phrase or to a paint one colour. Use this as an opportunity to ask God to fill you with his courage and lead you in the direction he's taking you. You could also write on balloons and then stamp on them as you pray for boldness.
6	God is in the whisper	1 Kings 19:11-13	Play Chinese whispers/ charades or Pictionary (one person starts knowing what the object or phrase is and everyone has to try and follow suit). It can be difficult to hear right. Remember that God wasn't in the wind, earthquake or fire (have sound effects for each). He was in the whisper.	Have a thirty second conversation with someone where the second person ignores what is being said (no facial expression etc). How does it feel when we cannot hear what is being communicated to us? How do we know when God speaks? What does it mean here when God doesn't speak in the wind, earthquake or fire (all ways he's spoken before)? When has God spoken to you in the whisper?	Write on some smooth pebbles the verse 'Be still and know that I am God' (Psalm 46:10). Spend time holding the pebble and being still and asking God what he is saying to you in this moment. This is something that you can take home.
7	Jesus is always with me	Matthew 28:16-20	Have a picture of a mountain. Think about what it would have been like to be on the mountainside with the risen Jesus.	Have we ever doubted? Why did some people doubt when Jesus was in front of them? How do we know that Jesus is always with us as we share our faith with others? What does that look like- use pictures of different locations e.g. park, workplace, school, dinner with friends, talking to kids, family outing. Choose one particular setting that you feel like you need to know Jesus is with you as you talk about him.	Have some blankets or scarves that people can wrap around their shoulders. Spend time praying for each individual that they would know God with them in everything they do. As you're physically wrapped up reflect on the verse 'you hem me in behind and before and you lay your hand upon me' (psalm 139:5). What does that mean as we follow the command to make disciples. Write down or draw the name/ picture of a person or some people you would like to share Jesus with. Use this as a reminder to pray for them and talk to them this week.
8	I am not ashamed	Romans 1:1-17	Who are you? Have a mirror and spend some time writing down or drawing what you think God sees. Paul totally knows his identity. He knows who he is and who he is, this means he doesn't need to be	What is the gospel? How would you share it? Spend time discussing this in pairs. In light of who you are and whose you are what is your story? How is God equipping you with courage to share your faith?	We can be brave and unashamed in the way we share the gospel with everyone. Write down your own story of how Jesus has given you courage and spoken to you in your life on helium balloons or paper aeroplanes and prayerful send these off as a celebration that

Appendix 7 – Accessible service plan

If you don't have a service sheet you could print out a few copies of a plan like this for the welcome team so that those who like to know what's going on can. Building in breaks and movement activities like those in this plan will help enable everyone the opportunity to participate no matter what their level of needs.

	Tea and coffee	You can choose a tea, coffee or another drink. This is time to chat to our friends.
	Pick up fidgets	Pick up a fidget and a shell, piece of tissue paper and cotton wool. Go and find a seat.
	Welcome	Tom will welcome everyone to church today.
	Worship	We will sing songs as worship to God. You can sit or stand or dance if you would like to.
	Prayer	Sarah will help everyone pray today. We can listen to what she says to God.
	Notices	Tom is going to tell us some dates for our diaries.
	Break	Tom will tell us when it's a break and we can move around or go to the toilet if we would like to.
	Talk- What is God saying to me right now?	Shell- Listen to the noise in the shell. God speaks to Elijah in a whisper.\n\nTissue paper- red and yellow like fire. God speaks to Moses in the fire of the burning bush.\n\nCotton wool- dreams. God speaks to Moses in a dream.
	Response- We hold our hands out to see what God would like to give us.	God wants to speak to you. See what he is saying to you today.
	Worship	We will sing more songs as worship to God.
	Tea and Coffee	You can choose to have a drink. You can chat to your friends.
	Finished	Church is finished, it is time to go home.

Appendix 8 – equipment recommendations

This is a list of equipment that might be useful and why it would be helpful. If you search online for the name of the equipment you should be able to find it for purchasing.

Piece of equipment	Use of equipment
Big point recordable button	Prayer button- This can be used to record a simple prayer which individuals can press to play. This enables individuals who do not have the language to say a whole prayer to participate. We would usually enable an individual to press the button, lay hands on them and pray over them one at a time in a group.
Move 'n' sit or circular wobble cushions	Movement (proprioceptive input) is really important. If an individual sits on one of these cushions which are filled with a bit of air they give the opportunity for moving even when sitting still.
Theraputty	Is resistive and is good for fidgeting with. Red is the medium soft colour, green is medium, blue is strong. You can choose which strength an individual may need. You can hide small objects (such as beads) in the putty. Looking for them gives good movement feedback and can be regulating. NB: putty will stick to hair, carpet and clothes, it comes off by sticking it to itself.
Tangles	These are great <u>fidgets</u> which enable individuals to get their body to a 'just right' level whilst listening. General rules around fidgets are that you tell individuals it's to help them concentrate and if they throw it you'll take it away.
Twist and lock blocks	
Therapy ball/ gym ball	A great way to give intense movement. The size of the ball depends on the distance between the floor and an individuals knee. You can bounce on a gym ball, roll over it on your tummy or backwards on your back.
Widget online symbols	Is a great piece of software which can be used to print symbols for your own context. You can also put your own photos into visual schedules or cards for discussions. *Please note we have used hand drawn symbols in this book as symbols are copyrighted.*
Whiteboards and whiteboard markers	Can be really useful within sessions, particularly if an individual is finding it difficult to understand a talk or teaching input you can draw out pictures or write key words to help support an individual to understand.
Ear defenders	Can help to block out background noise or reduce noise for those who have auditory sensitivity (ear plugs can work too). These can often make a big difference to being able to go into large scale worship events.
Clinical wipes	Are really useful to have for when equipment goes in mouths/ or gets dirty.
Chewy tube	A really useful piece of equipment for individuals who like to bite a lot. This can be a replacement for biting others or objects.
Sensory vibrating snake	This is a vibrating tube which can be really calming around an individual's neck or being held in their hands if they seek out a lot of touch feedback.
Lycra tunnel	A stretchy tunnel that gives a good amount of proprioceptive feedback.
Scooter board	You lie on this on your tummy and use your hands to propel yourself along. This can be really good for gaining more body awareness (proprioceptive feedback).
The accessible bible/ The bible project	The accessible bible is currently a new testament which uses the NIrV accessible version. The bible project has several videos and visual illustrations of bible passages.
Mini easy grip scissors	Easier to use scissors for craft activities for children that find cutting difficult.
Parachute, clay, giant jenga blocks (foam), blankets, paint, rice, baby lotion, shaving foam	Creative prayer activities enable individuals to connect with God through different parts of their sensory system. They may feel God's presence when they're feeling the wind of the parachute. They may know they can be bold by knocking down a tower of jenga blocks. They may explore what God is saying as they explore shaving foam.
Story box (fabric storage box with lid for children)	For multisensory stories- having a fold out story box which you cannot see into helps to increase motivation to engage if individuals need to come and look in your box for different parts of the story.
Exercise books	Prayer books- Are a way of recording what God is saying or speaking to each individual you're coming alongside. Particularly for individuals with limited communication this can be a really helpful way to show parents and carers what God has been saying.